Gaining Entrance Into Your Promised Land

by
Neil C. Ellis

Gaining Entrance Into Your Promised Land

by
Neil C. Ellis

PHOS PUBLISHING · INC
Tulsa, Oklahoma

Unless otherwise indicated, all Scripture quotations are taken from *The King James Version* of the Bible.

Gaining Entrance Into Your Promised Land
ISBN 0-9657706-5-6
Copyright © 1997 by
Neil C. Ellis, Senior Pastor
Mt. Tabor Full Gospel Baptist Church
P. O. Box N-9705
Nassau, Bahamas

Published by
Phos Publishing, Inc.
P. O. Box 690447
Tulsa, Oklahoma 74169-0447

Printed in the United States of America.

Contents

Dedication

This book is dedicated to all of the faithful and caring pastors, officers, and members of the Mount Tabor Full Gospel Baptist Church, whose inspiration and loyalty have given me impetus to dare such a study, and who, over the past ten years, have shown more interest in my teaching and preaching of the Word than I have had any right to hope for. May God forever be praised in the lives of these "Promised-Land Dwellers."

Preface

It is my personal conviction that many people who are members of the Body of Christ, are living beneath their individual potential. They are not taking advantage of all that God has ordained exclusively for them, primarily because of their ignorance of the principles recorded in God's Word. Consequently, Satan, with the help of all his demonic agents, is succeeding in keeping many of them away from entering into the "Land of Promise." The Word is still true: **Where there is no vision, the people perish...** (Proverbs 29:18).

In this study, I shall attempt, with the aid of the Holy Spirit, to give you spiritual truths and Biblical principles that I believe, when and if applied, will forever radically change your life and your walk with God.

Satan's intention is to paralyze your plan, abort your dreams, distract your mind and do whatever it takes to redirect your footsteps and prevent you from entering into the Land of Promise. But as you find victory and deliverance in your life, may the Lord, who has ordered me to the work of teaching and preaching His Word, find glory, honor, and praise in what I have attempted to share with you. Come on, let's go over into the Promised Land.

Foreword

by Bishop Eddie Long

The Bible records in Joshua 4:8 NKJV, **And the children of Israel did so, just as Joshua commanded, and took up twelve stones from the midst of the Jordan, as the Lord had spoken to Joshua, according to the number of the tribes of the children of Israel, and carried them over with them to the place where they lodged, and laid them down there.**

The reader must immediately notice that the children of Israel did *"just so,"* as the visionary Joshua instructed. They lent themselves as instruments of bidding to the man of God, understanding that God's man only performs what he hears from the Father. Key to entering the Promised Land is the ability to hear and follow the directives of God. Without the anointing of servitude, it is impossible to achieve what the Father has proposed.

Gaining Entrance Into Your Promised Land is an outstanding ministry tool for personal and group study. Bishop Neil Ellis gives detailed illumination to the truths of the Bible through this written teaching. There is a price to pay for God's blessings, and that price is *obedience*. The believer may ask, "Obedience to what?" His Word. "How do I know His Word? Who will discern the truth of His voice?" The leader plays an important part in a believer's relationship to God. A true leader must first have a personal relationship with God. Then, and only then, is he able to perform what he hears from the Father. There is no margin of error in such a leader because through relationship, his footsteps are ordered. The people can trust in such a leader, but will they?

Iniquity, deception, rebellion and sedition are all symptoms of sin sickness. This sickness is one that is summoned by the victim. Though sin is a summoned disease, it results in a demise of the carrier. God, in His mercy, may cause the cancerous death to be slow, presenting opportunities for repentance. But, sin unchecked will exact its wages and ultimately end in death. Second-guessing the man of God has its consequences, as with all sin. The promised blessings will ultimately be delayed or revoked.

Between the pages of this writing are truths which can help you avoid the mistakes of willful rebellion. Bishop Neil Ellis skillfully points out God's intentions for His people in this thoroughly researched, anointed writing. It is essential for all believers to enter a promised land. Key to our very existence is a willingness to receive from God at His appointed time. *Gaining Entrance Into Your Promised Land* can open your spirit to God's promised blessings and the level of submission required to receive them. Never before has a work been as thorough in its depth, yet simplistic in its presentation. This is a book that must be read by those who plan to walk in the fullness of the promises of God.

Bishop Eddie Long
Pastor, New Birth M. C. Church
Decatur, Georgia

1

Crossing Your Jordan

I sincerely believe that every Christian is entitled to a Promised-Land experience, not when we die and go to heaven, but right here on earth. However, in order to experience this lifestyle, we must come to the realization that there are instructions to follow, challenges to face and battles to be won. While every Christian is an "heir" to the Promised Land, only those following the instructions of the "will" would actually possess the promise. Our first consideration in this regard is discovering how to cross Jordan.

Through the years there has been an ongoing misconception in the Body of Christ of what the Promised Land in the Old Testament represents. Christians have sung songs and heard stories and preached sermons which have depicted the Promised Land as heaven. We talk of all the wonderful things that will happen when we get "over there."

This tragic misconception is very harmful. It has, in fact, kept countless thousands of believers living below the level of victory which God has designed for them. Promised Land dwelling is for every believer today. We can appreciate this when we understand what the types and shadows in the Old Testament are telling us. This book is designed to reveal these truths and bring all believers to a practical, present understanding of how to cross that river Jordan and enjoy the land flowing with milk and honey in this lifetime. We will also explore the pitfalls which the enemy has set to keep us from ever stepping our feet into that swollen river to cross over into the Promised Land.

Two Significant Crossings

We learn from the Old Testament of three important areas which the children of Israel experienced: Egypt, the wilderness, and last of all, the Promised Land. Between each there were two miraculous crossings. The first was across the Red Sea, the second was across the Jordan into the Promised Land.

The Jordan River serves as the eastern boundary of Canaan, and therefore serves as the eastern boundary of the Promised Land as well. The headwaters of this river originate from Lake Huleh. From there it flows into and out of the Sea of Galilee (or Sea of Gennesaret) and on down to the Dead Sea. It is the lowest depression on earth, thus the name, Jordan (Hebrew yarden), or "the descender."

This then was the place where the children of Israel had come to after wandering in the wilderness for forty years. The great walled city of Jericho is just a few miles on the other side, and the river which is presently at flood stage is flowing out of its banks. The Lord now gives them their marching orders. Just because the river was at flood stage didn't give them an excuse to sit down and quit.

> **And they commanded the people, saying, When ye see the ark of the covenant of the Lord your God, and the priests the Levites bearing it, then ye shall remove from your place, and go after it.**

And Joshua said unto the people, Sanctify yourselves: for to morrow the Lord will do wonders among you.

And it shall come to pass, as soon as the soles of the feet of the priests that bear the ark of the Lord, the Lord of all the earth, shall rest in the waters of Jordan, that the waters of Jordan shall be cut off from the waters that come down from above; and they shall stand upon an heap.

And as they that bare the ark were come unto Jordan, and the feet of the priests that bare the ark were dipped in the brim of the water, (for Jordan overfloweth all his banks all the time of harvest).

And the priests that bare the ark of the covenant of the Lord stood firm on dry ground in the midst of Jordan, and all the Israelites passed over on dry ground, until all the people were passed clean over Jordan.

Joshua 3:3,5,13,15,17

When the children of Israel came to the Jordan River, they had been in the wilderness for forty years. It's good to know if you are presently walking through a wilderness experience, that you are probably close to your Promised Land. This is no time to quit or slow down. Whenever you come to the end of your wilderness experience, it will always bring you right to the edge of your Jordan River. Once you get to the Jordan, the Promised Land is always in view.

But while the Promised Land is in view from the Jordan, it's not yet possessed. One of the things that God always gives you at the Jordan is "spiritual vision." When you make it through the wilderness and get to the Jordan, the Lord begins to unveil the things of God. He begins to give you spiritual foresight as to what could be yours if you just cross over the Jordan. Once you make it successfully through the wilderness and you end up at the Jordan, God will give you a glimpse of your Promised Land. But if you want to possess your Promised Land after your arrival at the Jordan, there's always one more step to take. You are required to follow the priests that bear the ark. You must move forward.

The book of Joshua is a demonstration of God's faithfulness. Here we learn that God led Israel into the land of Canaan just as He had previously led them out of the land of Egypt. In chapter 3 of Joshua, the children of Israel have been delivered from Pharaoh and have been brought out of Egypt, but they've still not made it into the Promised Land. It lies within striking distance, but they are not there yet.

It may be the same for some of us. The Promised Land may be close — we may even see some of the promises off in the distance — but we have not taken the next step necessary to cross over to receive them.

God's Instructions to Joshua

In Joshua, chapter 1, God calls Joshua and gives him specific instructions. When God calls someone, He will always give a specific assignment.

> **Moses my servant is dead; now therefore arise, go over this Jordan, thou, and all this people, unto the land which I do give to them, even to the children of Israel.**
>
> **Joshua 1:2**

Now we must understand that they have just come out of the wilderness. It's been a successful journey even though it took them thirty-nine years and eleven months longer than it was supposed to take. But they've finally come out of the wilderness. They're at the brink of the Jordan River. Moses had had a glimpse of the Promised Land and then he died because of disobedience. God then raised up his "assistant pastor," Joshua. And the first thing He says to him is "Arise!" He tells Joshua, "Get up!"

After going through the wilderness with all its pitfalls and problems, there was a temptation for them to sit down at the Jordan and rest a while. We used to sing a little song, a line of which said, "Sit down and rest a little while." But we have no time to sit down and rest. God can never do a great work with us until we "get up."

We must hear God saying, "Arise! Go over this Jordan." God is saying, "You're not yet in the Land of Promise. You must take one more step. Get up and go over Jordan." He told Joshua and the children of Israel, "If you will just cross over Jordan, there you will find the promises."

Challenges and Promises

God never gives a challenge unless He attaches a promise to it. The challenge was, "Get up and go over the Jordan." No matter that it was at flood stage. No matter that they had many people to move through. The challenge was to arise and go.

The promise was, "If you go over the Jordan, then every place your feet tread upon, I will give you."

> ...within three days ye shall pass over this Jordan, to go in to possess the land, which the Lord your God giveth you to possess it.
>
> **Joshua 1:11**

What Joshua and the children of Israel were to receive was determined by whether or not they got up. Some people have come through the wilderness, but then they simply sit down. God didn't just tell them to get up. He told them to cross over. God wanted them to know that He had nothing for them on that side of Jordan. They'd seen about all there was to see on the left side. God says, "Wherever you go, I'll give you the land, if you'll just lift up your heads and cross over" (Joshua 1:3).

The New Generation

In chapter 3 of Joshua, the children of Israel are no longer under the rulership of Pharaoh. They are no longer Egyptian slaves, but they still have not entered into the Promised-Land experience that God has in store for them.

We can clearly see the parallel in our lives today. Many Christians are saved and are free from sin, but they live defeated lives. There is no Promised-Land experience. There is no victory.

> **And Moses went up from the plains of Moab unto the mountain of Nebo, to the top of Pisgah, that is over against Jericho. And the Lord shewed him all the land of Gilead, unto Dan,**
>
> **And all Naphtali, and the land of Ephraim, and Manasseh, and all the land of Judah, unto the utmost sea,**
>
> **And the south, and the plain of the valley of Jericho, the city of palm trees, unto Zoar.**
>
> **And the Lord said unto him, This is the land which I sware unto Abraham, unto Isaac, and unto Jacob, saying, I will give it unto thy seed: I have caused thee to see it with thine eyes, but thou shalt not go over thither.**

> **So Moses the servant of the Lord died there in the land of Moab, according to the word of the Lord.**
>
> **Deuteronomy 34:1-5**

Moses couldn't see the Promised Land until he arrived at the Jordan. But he was at the Jordan long enough to get a long look. He was allowed to see what he could have had. It was as though the Lord said: "You listened to the people, and failed to listen to Me, Moses. I thank you for bringing them out of Egypt, through the wilderness to the Jordan. Now your work is finished. Joshua, come forth! A new leader is needed for a new generation."

While Moses and the Israelites were in the wilderness, they bore children. These children had now become mature adults and they became the new generation. Moses was out of touch with the new generation. Many of the people he was supposed to carry over had died in the wilderness. Joshua was raised up to take his place. In this day and time, we can all be a part of the new generation if we are ready to cross over into the Promised Land and possess it.

The Old Testament presents us with the types and shadows of the New Testament. The Old Testament is the "root," and the New Testament is the "fruit," so to speak. Today's churches should be the "fruit" since we are New Testament churches. We are the ones called to change our generation. We are the ones who should be exemplifying the Promised-Land experience.

We used to be a part of the Moses army which got as far as the Jordan. The Moses generation, the old order, celebrates coming out of Egypt and wandering around in the wilderness, arriving at the Jordan. But those of us who are changing our generation are the new nation — we are a part of the Joshua generation. We're the ones who are destined to go over into the Promised Land. We must take the next step!

Sanctification

When Joshua said to the people, Sanctify yourselves (Joshua 3:5), it certainly wasn't the first time the children of Israel had heard this admonition. They'd received that instruction many times before.

> For I am the Lord your God: ye shall therefore sanctify yourselves, and ye shall be holy...
>
> For I am the Lord that bringeth you up out of the land of Egypt, to be your God: ye shall therefore be holy, for I am holy.
>
> Leviticus 11:44,45
>
> Sanctify yourselves therefore, and be ye holy: for I am the Lord your God.
>
> And ye shall keep my statutes, and do them: I am the Lord which sanctify you.
>
> Leviticus 20:7,8

Nearly everything that had to do with the tabernacle had to be sanctified, or "set apart" for use in worship unto the Lord. This setting apart applied to the people as well. As we can see from the passage in Leviticus 20, it is a dual operation. We are to sanctify ourselves, but God also is involved. He promises to sanctify us.

In Hebrews 13 we find that in the New Testament, sanctification involved the shed blood of Jesus:

> Wherefore Jesus also, that he might sanctify the people with his own blood, suffered without the gate.
>
> Hebrews 13:12

Sanctification then has to do with holy living. Those who camp by the Jordan and stay there don't believe in sanctification. They believe they can do whatever they want, and then say, "God's grace is sufficient for me." They live as though God's grace will cover premeditated sin. But God says, "I want this new generation to sanctify themselves."

Between the wilderness and the Promised Land, there is the Jordan. But before crossing the Jordan, there must be sanctification. Why? Because the enemy is "terrified of the sanctified."

Notice that God didn't tell them to prepare the ammunition to fight their way into the Promised Land. They didn't need to concern themselves with guns or military gear. We don't need that either.

The last part of the fifth verse of Joshua, chapter 3, says, "For tomorrow the Lord will do wonders among you." God wanted them to know He was getting ready to surprise them with miracles.

When we come to our Jordan and sanctify ourselves, then God takes us to levels we've never seen before. The record is, **Eye hath not seen, nor ear heard, neither have entered into the heart of man, the things which God hath prepared for them that love him** (1 Corinthians 2:9).

God may be telling you this very moment, "You've been faithful for a long time. I've seen your tears. I've heard your prayers. If you can hold on until tomorrow, I'm getting ready to work wonders."

But before God can do His part, we must do ours: *Jordan must be crossed*. You must take one more step. You may be at the brink of receiving the greatest harvest you've ever received since the day of your salvation.

Jordan — A Place of Warfare

The Jordan River is known for many historic events in the Bible, the best known of which is the baptism of Jesus. But the Jordan has special significance other than being the place of Jesus' baptism. It also has significance other than being the place where the children of Israel crossed over into the Promised Land. The Jordan has always been a *place of pain, a place of opposition* and *a place of great difficulty.*

Judges 3:28 describes a battle fought at the Jordan. Again in Judges 12:5, we will observe that yet another great battle was fought at the Jordan. Why is there so much warfare at the Jordan? Why is the Jordan a place of great difficulty? Because it's the devil's final opportunity to prevent you from entering into your Promised Land. The enemy must fight at this point. He must somehow do whatever it takes in order to prevent you from taking the next step, because he knows that if you ever cross your Jordan, it's over for him!

There is a Promised-Land experience that God has for each and every believer. It's simply not true that God wills for you to be down and out while here on earth — while you're waiting to get to heaven. You don't have to wait for the sweet by-and-by. You can experience your Promised Land here and now. It was no one other than Jesus Himself who told us that when we pray, we ought to say:

> **...Our Father which art in heaven, Hallowed be thy name. Thy kingdom come. Thy will be done in earth, as it is in heaven.**
>
> **Matthew 6:9,10**

You don't have to wait until the undertaker rolls you out of the church to possess the Promised Land. God's Word promises us a type of heaven here on earth. But God is asking you to take *one more step*!

Flood Season

Joshua 3:15 says, **And as they that bare the ark were come unto Jordan, and the feet of the priests that bare the ark were dipped in the brim of the water, (for Jordan overfloweth all his banks all the time of harvest).** This verse may give insight as to why you've been going through such difficulty. Perhaps you've been in a place where every time you get over one problem, here comes another. Perhaps for you it seems as if as soon as God delivers you in one area, problems arise in another area.

When they arrived at the Jordan, it was at harvesttime when the river was at flood stage.

• The children of Israel were eager to enter the Promised Land.

• They were eager to live in peace.

• They were eager to conquer new nations.

But here they stood at the edge of the Jordan which lies between them and the Promised Land. Now, observe very carefully: Here they are at the Jordan River and the water is overflowing its banks. God sees to it that they arrive at the river right at flood season. It is the worst possible time for them to attempt to cross the Jordan, yet God instructs them to cross! When God is getting ready to do something great, usually He does it in the face of great odds.

Many Christians are bewildered as they approach the Jordan and they end up at the Jordan of their lives at flood stage. There are problems on the job, problems at home, problems with the neighbors, problems at church. What's happening? You're at the Jordan and it's flood season. Flood season!

When we come out of the bondage of our Egypt and successfully make our way through the wilderness, we always end up at the Jordan River. But as we approach the Jordan, Satan turns up the heat and declares war. It is at this point that some Christians choose this spot to sit down and say, *"I can't go any further. I can't take any more. This is too much for me."*

But this is no time to quit. You've come too far. You've toiled too long. You're too close to the Promised Land. If you will take just one more step, you'll make it over the Jordan.

Don't let the enemy get you sidetracked. It took the children of Israel forty years to get to Jordan by way of the wilderness. The Bible says they "wandered" about in the wilderness — they didn't travel in a straight line directly to Jordan.

The devil tried his best to defeat them before they could ever reach the Jordan. That's why one entire generation died before they ever saw the Promised Land. There was no way the devil wanted that large group of people who came out of slavery to cross over the Jordan into the Promised Land. So he kept them sidetracked — wandering.

No Bridges Over Jordan

You may be at the Jordan where you can actually see your Promised Land. But between you and the

Promised Land is the Jordan River. God will not put a bridge over your Jordan. To get over you must fight. You must take the next step.

But please note, it's here that God will give the spiritual visions of that with which He wants to bless His children. But we must want it bad enough to fight back and defeat the devil on every level. It's here that we must remember that the same God who parted the Red Sea, can also part the Jordan River. And your Jordan is always smaller in comparison to your Red Sea.

Comparing the Crossings

The Red Sea was twelve miles wide. Where the children of Israel crossed, it may have been less, but not much. We do know that it was wide enough to drown the entire army of Pharaoh in it. The average depth was from 2,500 to 3,500 feet. The parting of the waters of the Red Sea was an incredible miracle.

Now the width of the Jordan was between 45 feet and approximately 75 feet. And the depth of the Jordan was between 6 and 12 feet. Think of the difference between the depths of the Red Sea and the Jordan River. There's no comparison. But there they were crying and complaining at the Jordan which was much smaller than the Red Sea that God had already brought them over.

This is good news for believers. The trouble that's facing us now is nothing compared to what we've been through already. We need only think back one year — think how far the Lord has brought you! Think of the things from which you've already been delivered. Stop and look where you are now. Then remember this:

The same God who brought you through your Red

Sea can surely get you over your Jordan River. If God brought you out of Egypt, He can surely lead you into the Promised Land. If God saved your soul, He can surely deal with your present problems. If God saved you from destruction, can He not handle your little dilemma? If God changed your heart, I know He can change your home. If God changed your outlook, He can change your outcome. If God fixed up your yesterday, He can handle your today, and give you hope for your tomorrow.

Time To Cross

But Satan wants you to give up at the Jordan. Because if you take one more step, you'll get into the Promised Land! It's time to take a stand and declare, "I don't care what it takes, *I'm crossing over!*" You may have to praise your way over. You may have to shout your way over. You may have to pray your way over. But make up your mind you are going over. The Promised Land is going to be your new dwelling place. You may not have a dime in your pocket, you may be facing the biggest challenge of your life, but you can cross over. Just take one more step.

Begin to envision what you've been praying for all these months, all these years. Begin to see yourself in the Promised Land. No one can steal your Promised Land. It belongs to you. It's your heritage. God said wherever you tread, He will give that land to you — a land that flows with milk and honey. Milk represents the necessities, and honey represents the bonuses. This means that once you cross over the Jordan and make it into the Promised Land, not only will you have all your needs met, but God will also give you some of what you want! God will give you what you need, and He

will also add in some of what you want. The Bible is
still true!

> Trust in the Lord, and do good; so shalt thou
> dwell in the land, and verily thou shalt be fed.

> Delight thyself also in the Lord; and he shall give
> thee the desires of thine heart.

> **Psalm 37:3,4**

Dwelling in the Promised Land will allow you to
have the desires of your heart fulfilled. Keep in mind
that dwelling in the Promised Land demands that we
change our mind-set. We can't take the old mind-set
which we had in Egypt — which was a slave mentality
— and survive in the Promised Land.

> And be not conformed to this world: but be ye
> transformed by the renewing of your mind....

> **Romans 12:2**

Stop thinking that God meant for you to be poor.
If He meant for you to be poor, He would have left you
as a slave in bondage in Egypt. God wants you to enjoy
life here on earth. He wants to give us the Kingdom in
this life.

Summary

There is a Promised-Land experience for every
believer, but we must want it enough to press into the
warfare that the enemy will throw at us. No matter how
bad things look, if God was able to redeem your soul
and save you from an eternal hell, then He is well able
to part the waters and guide you across the Jordan
into your Promised-Land experience. The wilderness
may have been a mammoth challenge, but the bank of
the Jordan is no place to sit down and complain and

certainly no place to quit. God gives the admonition to cross over and possess your Promised Land.

2

Deception in the Promised Land

God Orders Us To Cross Jordan

> Hear, O Israel: Thou art to pass over Jordan this day, to go in to possess nations greater and mightier than thyself, cities great and fenced up to heaven,
>
> A people great and tall, the children of the Anakims, whom thou knowest, and of whom thou hast heard say, Who can stand before the children of Anak!
>
> Understand therefore this day, that the Lord thy God is he which goeth over before thee; as a consuming fire he shall destroy them, and he shall bring them down before thy face: so shalt thou drive them out, and destroy them quickly, as the Lord hath said unto thee.
>
> Deuteronomy 9:1-3

From this passage we see clearly that the Lord's instruction to the children of Israel was for them to cross over the Jordan. And not only to cross over, but to cross over and then possess the land.

Yet another verse in Deuteronomy echoes this admonition:

> For ye shall pass over Jordan to go in to possess the land which the Lord your God giveth you, and ye shall possess it, and dwell therein.
>
> Deuteronomy 11:31

In the last chapter we learned that this is the place where the enemy will fight the hardest — Jordan is a place of warfare. There's no way the devil wants Christians to be entering into this wonderful Land of Promise.

Many Christians are at the Jordan and are at the point of giving up. The wilderness was difficult enough, but now it seems as though the enemy is throwing everything he has at us. He intensifies his fight in order to stop Christians from crossing over the Jordan. But we must stand firm, sanctify ourselves according to God's Word and step by step cross over the Jordan and go on in to the Promised Land.

Promised Land for Every Believer

It's important to note that the Promised Land was there for every person who left Egypt under Moses' leadership. It was accessible to every one of them. But one entire generation died in the wilderness and never made it in. See to it that you are not added to this list!

> For the Lord thy God bringeth thee into a good land, a land of brooks of water, of fountains and depths that spring out of the valleys and hills;
>
> A land of wheat, and barley, and vines, and fig trees, and pomegranates; a land of oil olive, and honey;
>
> A land wherein thou shalt eat bread without scarceness, thou shalt not lack any thing in it; a land whose stones are iron, and out of whose hills thou mayest dig brass.
>
> **Deuteronomy 8:7-9**

After we cross the Jordan, we are promised that we will find water. Plenty of water. This is a good land, we are told. A land of brooks of water, of fountains and depths that spring out of valleys and hills.

Water was one of the primary things lacking in the wilderness. For a million people in the desert, water is a vital commodity. But in the Promised Land, the Bible says there's water all over the place — in the valleys, on top of the hills, from the brooks, and from the fountains.

This is symbolic of the fact that whatever we lacked in the times of our personal wilderness experiences, we will have in abundance once we cross Jordan. That's why He said, we'll not just live, but we will multiply in the Promised Land. Whatever the situations that gave you trouble while you were in the wilderness, once you cross over Jordan into the Promised Land, expect those situations to be the first areas for God to move in a mighty way just to prove that the devil is a liar.

If you are struggling with your marriage in the wilderness, then new romance and new fire are about to break loose in your marriage once you enter into the Promised Land. If you had problems with your finances, that will be the first area of victory for you in the Promised Land. Whatever area the enemy attacked you in while going through the wilderness, expect God to bless you in that realm to an even greater degree. Stand back and watch God do wonders among you. Scripture says there is an abundance of wheat and barley, and vines, and fig trees, and pomegranates; a land of oil olive, and honey. We can "eat bread without scarceness." *Bread* here represents food, period.

That means you can have food and enough to spare; you will never run out. You can be giving food away because you will have so much. You may have had to settle for chicken in the wilderness, now you will have steak and lobster. You may have had to settle for corned beef in the wilderness, but now it's time to set the table for plenty. And you'll need more than a fork and knife. You'll need salad forks, soup spoons, and cocktail forks. You can have food without scarceness! God's Word says so. It's time to settle it in our spirits, because we've been suffering too long.

This is the time when you will eat peanut butter and jelly sandwiches, but only because you feel like it, not because you have to. Or corned beef because you choose to, not because you must. You will have more than you need. You may not have it in the cupboard yet, but it's in the Promised Land. You may not have it in your house yet, but it's in the Promised Land and you're a Promised-Land dweller. As long as you're in the land and the food is in the land, it belongs to you.

Thou shalt not lack any thing in [the land]. That's what the Word says. This helps us to see why we have so much warfare at the Jordan. That's why Satan tries to keep us at the Jordan.

We used to sing a song that said: "I'm waiting down here at the river till You come, Lord Jesus." That's poor theology, because we have no time to wait at the river till Jesus comes. He's already told us to arise, get up, and cross over. He wants us to "occupy" until He comes, not "wait."

But the devil knows that after we've been delivered and get to the point where we don't need to depend on anybody to give us anything, that's freedom! That's liberty! He is not eager to see that happen.

The devil wants you on the left side of Jordan where you can't get a job. Or if you are working, you're only making minimum wage and living in lack. He wants to keep you living a defeated life in order for him to be able to operate your life via remote control!

Possess the Land

When we cross over, all the promises listed in Deuteronomy, chapter 8, belong to us. We're going to have the water, the wheat, the barley and bread without scarceness. We are to go in and possess it.

Deuteronomy 9:1 tells us we will **...possess nations greater and mightier than thyself....** Nations. That doesn't mean a little island, but nations. This represents everything that while you were on the other side of Jordan, was outside of your reach. This represents everything that you couldn't obtain on the other side of Jordan because you were not qualified.

You know that the enemy told you that you weren't good enough. But you also know that God said if you arise, take one more step and cross over the Jordan, things will be different. For example, if you went on a job interview recently and were turned down, make another appointment. When you show up for the interview, God will begin to put words in your mouth that will make the interviewer forget what everyone who came before you said, and everybody who will come after you says as well. On the application it may say, "Bachelor's degree preferred." But perhaps when you finished high school you had no means to go further. Maybe you barely finished high school — you weren't saved yet and you hardly passed anything.

But lo and behold, you got saved. Then you learned about Promised-Land living. Now while everybody's at night school looking for their little bachelor's degree, you'll be making a good salary. Because when you get into the Promised Land, God will give you nations — not just what you're qualified for, but things that are beyond your qualifications. That's God!

In Deuteronomy 9, verse 1, He said that He'll give you **cities great and fenced up to heaven**. That means there was no way you could get what you longed to obtain because the fence was too high.

These cities represent every door that was previously closed in your face while you were on the other side of Jordan. All you need to do is think back about every door that was shut in your face before you crossed over. You'll remember this door over here and that door over there. But now God says, "I don't care how high the fence was, I'm pulling it down. I'm letting you go in. When you come to the city that they closed in your face, you'll walk right up and take what belongs to you."

This passage from Deuteronomy 9 says God will give us nations and cities, but it also says one other thing. It refers to the **people great and tall, the children of the Anakims...** (v. 2). This represents the people who have always had the upper hand over you. Before you crossed over to the Promised Land, they were the head, and you were the tail.

There may have been a supervisor who treated you poorly just because he didn't know how to handle power. You know why that supervisor treated you like that? Because he was given a glimpse of your potential. He played the devil's advocate, saying, "Look here, I need to put stumbling blocks in her/his way to make sure she/he doesn't get this promotion. Because she'll/he'll get a little closer to my job, and I know what she's/he's capable of doing. If I make her/him look good, if I give her/him a good reference, if I give her/him the right evaluation that she/he should get, the boss may move me out and put her/him in."

My advice to you is: *Get ready anyhow!* Remember, you're in the Promised Land and God gives the Anakims into your hand.

God Goes Before Us

God has promised that He will go into the Land of Promise before we do. He goes forth as a **consuming fire** (Deuteronomy 9:3), to destroy the great and tall people who dwell there. He says he will bring them down before your face. Now, with a promise like that, we would be fools if we came into the Promised Land and tried to fight our own battle.

> **For the weapons of our warfare are not carnal, but mighty through God to the pulling down of strong holds.**
>
> **2 Corinthians 10:4**

We are never admonished by God to fight in our own strength or under our own power. That's why God gave the instruction for sanctification before the time of crossing over. We stay in faith, we remain sanctified, and God promises not only to help us go across. But He will go over before us.

We are to keep our eyes on the priest. When the priest steps into the water, follow the priest. When we're crossing, He makes His way through the crowd to get in front of you. And when He gets in front He goes in with fire. All we have to do is cross. We don't fight, we just cross. We don't get discouraged on the banks of the Jordan, we just cross. We don't listen to the critics, we cross.

What is the purpose of the consuming fire? To destroy the enemies who dwell there. Those enemies that we left behind as we crossed the Jordan — they have partners. But God waits until we reach the Promised Land, then He lines them up in front of us and destroys them. God never "shows off" until the enemies show up.

Remember what David said?

> Thou preparest a table before me in the presence of mine enemies....
>
> **Psalm 23:5**

He doesn't prepare the table until the enemies are "present." The devil is a liar, a loser, and a deceiver. He tried to hold you back from crossing Jordan, but he failed. When he fails at the Jordan, that means he must have representatives in the Promised Land. They are there to ensure that you do not benefit from the Promised Land after arriving there!

Now how can there be enemies there if this is a Land of Promise? The same way Satan can get into the church. The same way Satan came to be in the presence of God in Job, chapter 1. God allows Satan to do certain things.

The Weapon of Deception

Before we reach the Promised Land, the enemy can lie to us and tell us there's nothing there. But once we arrive, he must use a new ploy, a new strategy — deception. Once you are in sight of the promises, you can see the grapes and the milk and honey, he will attempt to deceive you into believing that you can't really possess anything that is there. That is when the devil will throw up to you your "corned beef" days. He says,

"Look at you. You're nothing. You know steak is not for you. You can't digest it." He says, "Look at you driving that broken-down car that runs hot. Every night it breaks down on the same street. And every time you turn it off, you need a jump to get it started again. So how do you think now in the Promised Land that a Lincoln Continental belongs to you?" He messes with your mind. And if you listen to him, you'll come to the point where you eventually agree with him.

The truth is, if you're sanctified, and if you made it across the Jordan — **no good thing will he withhold from them that walk uprightly** (Psalm 84:11). If we are not on our guard, when we get into the Promised Land, we'll still be living a defeated life. Right in the middle of the Promised Land we can be defeated! Deception is one of the devil's biggest weapons.

The Weapon of Discouragement

Next to the weapon of deception comes the weapon of discouragement. Once the enemy convinces us that we're not qualified for all the wonderful promises, then we slump to the ground and pout because things are not working for us! "I thought I was supposed to be in the Promised Land, but nothing is working like God told me it would." And right in the midst of the promises, we are overcome with discouragement.

Going Backward

There is something very significant that happens when we succumb to the enemy's wiles in our Promised Land. If we are not careful when we arrive in the Promised Land, we will soon be back over Jordan — right back where we started. There's nothing more agonizing than living a defeated life in the Promised Land. Here's what can happen. You're in the Promised Land and all your friends and family members who came over with you, are living like kings. And you're still doing without. That can be devastating. If you don't begin immediately to take authority when you get in the Promised Land, you're in for some tough days.

The first thing to do when you make it out of the wilderness and cross the Jordan into the Promised Land is "take authority." Because the demonic forces that have specific assignments there will drive you out of your Promised-Land experience. And be aware of this: going back across the Jordan is worse than crossing over the first time.

> **For if after they have escaped the pollutions of the world through the knowledge of the Lord and Saviour Jesus Christ, they are again entangled therein, and overcome, the latter end is worse with them than the beginning.**
>
> **For it had been better for them not to have known the way of righteousness, than, after they have known it, to turn from the holy commandment delivered unto them.**
>
> **2 Peter 2:20,21**

The First Promised Land

This is what happened to Adam and Eve. The Garden called Eden was their Promised Land. Everything they needed was in the Promised Land. But the enemy saw it and guess what he did — he deceived Eve. Adam failed to cover Eve, and she was deceived. Therefore, they were put out of the Garden. SOMEBODY WHO DIDN'T BELONG IN THE PROMISED LAND PUT OUT THE PROMISED-LAND INHABITERS.

Let's bring this up into our lives today. God places some people in our lives, and so does the devil. That's why we must be careful who we go to lunch with. I'm not talking about dating; I'm talking about co-workers. The devil can send people on your job to drive you out of your Promised Land. God gave you that job, and you're supposed to be going higher and higher. Promotion comes from God.

> **For promotion cometh neither from the east, nor from the west, nor from the south.**
>
> **But God is the judge: he putteth down one, and setteth up another.**
>
> **Psalm 75:6,7**

The devil will bring in a co-worker or two and they may be talking defeat. They may be gossiping. They may be talking about matters that are not edifying to your spirit. It can distract you from what God's getting ready to do with you and for you. In effect, they can drive you out of your Promised Land.

Dwellers in the Promised Land must be alert and on guard.

Determine that you're not going to go back. Gone should be the days when the devil could scare you off with his roar. The devil's not going to quit, but you can't quit either.

- The Promised Land belongs to you.
- All the benefits belong to you.
- Healing and health belong to you.
- Riches, wealth and prosperity belong to you.
- Abundant life belongs to you.

- If you're married, you're not supposed to have just a "marriage," but in the Promised Land you'll have a good marriage.
  - A productive career belongs to you.
  - A good name belongs to you.

Whatever it was that the enemy stole from you before you came into the Promised Land, it's time to take it back. Christianity and poverty are not synonymous. They don't go together. Christianity and prosperity go together. God's plan for believers is for them to prosper even as their soul prospers (3 John 2).

Summary

God may order us to cross over Jordan, but the enemy is ready to thwart us by using deception and discouragement. If we are ignorant of his devices, we will find ourselves being driven out of our Promised Land, just as Adam and Eve were driven from the Garden of Eden. It's not a part of God's plan for us to retreat, but to press forward and possess the land.

3

Taking Authority in the Promised Land

Making the Enemy Tremble

In the last chapter we discussed the fact that the enemy plans to defeat us once we arrive in our Promised Land. In spite of that, the Lord instructs us to stand our ground, and possess the land. Then in Joshua, chapter 5, God gives us a glimpse into the realm of the enemy. This passage should put hope and courage in your heart.

> **And it came to pass, when all the kings of the Amorites, which were on the side of Jordan westward, and all the kings of the Canaanites, which were by the sea, heard that the Lord had dried up the waters of Jordan from before the children of Israel, until we were passed over, that their heart melted, neither was there spirit in them any more, because of the children of Israel.**
>
> **Joshua 5:1**

Another version of this verse says, **Their hearts failed, and there was no courage left in them**. Yet another version says, **They were disheartened and lost courage at their approach**. Here we see that the enemy's heart is melting because of the children of Israel. When we know who we are and what belongs to us, it should make the enemy tremble.

Take a close look at the following verse:

> **But the saints of the most High shall take the kingdom, and possess the kingdom for ever, even for ever and ever.**
>
> **Daniel 7:18**

Taking and possessing the land is part of God's plan for each of His children. If, because of reading the first two chapters of this book, you've made the quality decision to cross over into the Promised Land, you are now a Promised-Land dweller. Because of that, the enemy is trembling.

We learned from Deuteronomy, chapter 8, verses 7 and 9, that we will lack nothing in the Promised Land. Now what happens after we dwell in that land for a time?

God Is in the Multiplication Business

> **When thou hast eaten and art full, then thou shalt bless the Lord thy God for the good land which he hath given thee.**
>
> **Beware that thou forget not the Lord thy God, in not keeping his commandments, and his judgments, and his statutes, which I command thee this day:**
>
> **Lest when thou hast eaten and art full, and hast built goodly houses, and dwelt therein;**
>
> **And when thy herds and thy flocks multiply, and thy silver and thy gold is multiplied, and all that thou hast is multiplied;**
>
> **Then thine heart be lifted up, and thou forget the Lord thy God, which brought thee forth out of the land of Egypt, from the house of bondage.**
>
> **Deuteronomy 8:10-14**

There is a key word in this passage which is critical to understanding how serious God is about our Promised-Land experience. That is the word *when*. This is our assurance that these promises are certain, and we're to bless God for giving us this good land. There's nothing we can do to deserve such blessings. It wasn't because of our intelligence, nor was it because of our own righteousness. The Word tells us that our righteousness is as filthy rags (Isaiah 64:6). Our Promised-Land dwelling is due solely because of God's mercy and grace, and we are to bless the Lord for it.

The Scripture says, "*When* we have eaten and are full." That means as long as we are in the Promised Land, we can't starve...we won't starve. Everything that you lacked on the other side of Jordan, you can get it in the Promised Land. If that is not so, then you might as well have never crossed the Jordan.

It says, "*When* thou hast built goodly houses." Notice, "houses" is plural. God is trying to tell you that within your lifetime you may move once or twice. If you're living in a less-than-desirable house now, God will get you out of that one and into a better one. If you're paying rent, God wants to get you out of there and into your own home — because He said, "*When*"! God wants to bring you to the place where you are growing from glory to glory (2 Corinthians 3:18).

If this had said, "goodly homes," the connotation would have been different. But He says "houses." He's talking about buildings. If you are planning to apply for a loan on a house and people have been telling you that you're not qualified — now is the time. Because now you know God can give you things you never qualified for on the other side of Jordan. You're in the Promised Land, so it's just a matter of time.

We will build goodly houses and live in them. That means if you go to the bank to borrow money to build your house, you will live in the house and the bank can't take it. In the Promised Land, the bank can't take your house. You will live in it. You *will* live in it and be able to maintain it and meet the payments.

Verse 13 of Deuteronomy, chapter 8, says your herds and flocks will multiply, along with your gold and silver. Christians who think they have to be poor just because they're saved, do not understand Promised-Land dwelling. This is good news for those Christians who aren't used to having anything. If you're not used to having nice things, these promises are difficult for you to fathom. But in the Promised Land, everything that God has belongs to His children. It's time to tell yourself: "When"!

It's time we took God's Word and used it as our authority. We aren't considering what might happen "if" our gold and silver are multiplied. The word is *when* our gold and silver are multiplied — *when* our money is multiplied back to us.

If that were all this scripture passage promised, we would be greatly blessed. But look what else it says: **And all that thou hast is multiplied.** Begin to thank God for your increase because God is definitely in the multiplying business!

Power To Get Wealth

But thou shalt remember the Lord thy God: for it is he that giveth thee power to get wealth, that he

> may establish his covenant which he sware unto thy
> fathers, as it is this day.
> **Deuteronomy 8:18**

This promise of power to get wealth, found in verse
18, makes me wonder why some Christians try to tell
me I should apologize because I have a little something.
Yet it's God who gives me the power to get wealth. This
is no time to apologize; it's time to rejoice. He gives
power to get wealth for a reason: *that He may establish
His covenant*. When God blesses us, He wants us to turn
around and bless others. He doesn't bless us so we can
show off our bankbooks and talk about our possessions.
He blesses us, then He puts some people around us
whose breakthrough depends on our gift(s). When
we bless others, they, in return, should turn around
and bless others, which keeps it moving right on down
the line.

> And God is able to make all grace abound
> toward you; that ye, always having all sufficiency in
> all things, may abound to every good work...
>
> Being enriched in every thing to all bounti-
> fulness, which causeth through us thanksgiving to
> God.
> **2 Corinthians 9:8,11**

Passing the blessing along creates a spirit of thanksgiving to God. Another version says when the saints
give, it results in *many cries of thanksgiving to God*. From
that blessing which you initiated, it comes back to you
many times. Stinginess is like a disease, and poverty
can be as bad as cancer.

Different Than Egypt

> For the land, whither thou goest in to possess it,
> is not as the land of Egypt, from whence ye came out,

out, where thou sowedst thy seed, and wateredst it
with thy foot, as a garden of herbs.

Deuteronomy 11:10

This reference to the foot meant they were forced
to use a treadmill in order to draw water or transport
water to irrigate the fields and gardens. The connotation is that it involved a great deal of work. But the
Promised Land is not like Egypt; nor is it like the
wilderness. We're in the Promised Land, and we must
act accordingly.

God Is the Caretaker

But the land, whither ye go to possess it, is a
land of hills and valleys, and drinketh water of the
rain of heaven:

A land which the Lord thy God careth for: the
eyes of the Lord thy God are always upon it, from the
beginning of the year even unto the end of the year.

Deuteronomy 11:11,12

God is the Caretaker of the Promised Land. He does
all the sowing; He does all the watering; He does all the
fertilizing; He does all the harvesting.

And it shall come to pass, if ye shall hearken
diligently unto my commandments which I command
you this day, to love the Lord your God, and to serve
him with all your heart and with all your soul,

That I will give you the rain of your land in his
due season, the first rain and the latter rain, that thou
mayest gather in thy corn, and thy wine, and thine
oil.

Deuteronomy 11:13,14

Note the words in this passage, *due season*. Every
Christian has a *due season*, and we must learn not to

become envious of others who are in the midst of their due season. If you become envious in the midst of somebody else's due season, when your due season comes around, you may still be bound by the spirits of envy and jealousy. That attitude could cause your due season to pass you right by. We must learn to rejoice and be glad when others are in the midst of their *due season*.

Understand that before God blesses them again, your time must come around. Declare that your *due season* is coming, and then rejoice with others who are in their *due season*. Keep in mind, you cannot reap before your *due season*.

> And let us not be weary in well doing: for in due season we shall reap, if we faint not.
>
> Galatians 6:9

Perhaps you've been sowing for months and it seems like nothing is happening. The devil is trying to tell you to stop tithing and use that money for something else. But there's a due season, and you can't reap before your due season. Your due season is on the way, and it's nearer than it was yesterday! If you hold out and faint not, your due season is right around the corner!

Be Strong; Be Courageous

> Therefore shall ye keep all the commandments which I command you this day, that ye may be strong, and go in and possess the land, whither ye go to possess it;
>
> And that ye may prolong your days in the land, which the Lord sware unto your fathers to give unto

them and to their seed, a land that floweth with milk
and honey.

Deuteronomy 11:8,9

This is land where things "flow." Nothing was flowing in the wilderness. Remember, there was no water.
Moses had to strike the rock to supply the needed
water. But now, in the Promised Land, milk and honey
flow. As mentioned previously, the milk refers to your
necessities. The honey represents the little extras that
God supplies. In the book of Ruth, the gleaners were
instructed to leave **handfuls of purpose for her** (Ruth
2:16). This extra grain represents the extras the Lord
enjoys supplying for His children. There were no frills
or "extras" in the wilderness. Only the necessities. But
now in the Promised Land, both necessities and extras
are supplied.

In verse 8, of Deuteronomy, chapter 11, Promised-
Land dwellers are given the same admonition that
God gave to Joshua before he took the people across
the Jordan. He told Joshua, **Be strong and of a good
courage** (Joshua 1:9). Likewise, He tells the children of
Israel to "be strong." This doesn't refer to physical
strength, but rather to being courageous. It means to
take authority!

Why do people in the Promised Land need to be
strong? Because we will come up against situations in
which we must be prepared to take authority. Satan will
be there at every turn, attempting to shorten our stay in
the Promised Land.

At the Jordan, Satan made sure you knew he
was the enemy who did not want you to cross over.
However, in the Promised Land, he will be disguised.
He can't come at you and try to tell you there is no

Promised Land. You're already in it. You can see the milk and honey for yourself. His tactics must be altered. Rather than tell you there is no Promised Land, now he tells you it's not for you. He must use deception. You're not qualified for all this bounty. The enemy says to you, "You know you're a corned beef type of person. Your mother grew up on corned beef. Your grandma grew up on corned beef. And you are a corned beef person. What do you think you're doing with lobster? You know you can't digest it."

Now I'm using an example in the food realm, but it can be in any realm. It's the enemy's ploy to mess with your mind and keep you thinking small, to keep you thinking defeat and failure.

Pretty soon you'll start saying, "That's true. I did grow up on corned beef. I guess I'm just a corned beef person."

Remember, when you're living in the Promised Land, you can eat corned beef if that's what you want. But you don't eat corned beef because that's all you've got. The Bible says you will lack *nothing*. There's lobster in the Promised Land — and lamb chops, barbecued ribs, steak and shrimp. It's there in abundance.

Stand Your Ground

As Promised-Land dwellers, we must be vigilant. We must be alert. We must stand our ground and take authority. After coming through the wilderness and crossing over the Jordan, we must not back down or give in, because the devil won't quit. He doesn't even belong in the land. God gave it to you and me. Now we must take authority.

We learned from Joshua 5:1 that the enemy in the land is scared. **...Their heart melted, neither was there spirit in them any more....**

The enemy dwelling in the land heard that God parted the Jordan and it frightened them. "We didn't expect them to come over," they said. "We knew the Jordan was between us and them, and it was flood season. How did they get over here?" They could hardly believe the report. It was a terrifying report.

This is why the Lord gives us Scripture to tell us to simply take the authority. Their enemies are running scared; their hearts have *already* melted. Their spirits are *already* broken and they are frightened. The fear of God is on them because they heard how God parted the Jordan. Now the truth is, the enemies aren't actually afraid of the children of Israel, or God's children today. Rather, they are afraid of the God who is using them. God already promised He would go before us and put fear in the hearts of the inhabitants there.

Don't Be Bothered By the Noise

We learn in 1 Peter 5:8 that the devil goes about as a **roaring lion**. The enemy has the noise. Their hearts have melted, the Word says, and their spirits are gone, but they still have a mouth.

Now when you show up in the Promised Land, all they have to do is try to scare you off. They will attempt to scare you because that's the only ammunition they have. The enemy is merely trying to see if you will pick up and move out.

The enemy in the Promised Land is trying to scare you away from getting what belongs to you. All the enemy needs to do is see if you will run off. If he ever hears you say "boo" back, guess who will break off running? They will!

So, as Promised-Land dwellers, we're armed with knowledge and we're armed with the Word. Whenever they come after you, whoever roars the loudest, goes on in. They know what's yours. They know it belongs to you. They know you're qualified. And they are actually scared of you.

Once you understand the position of the enemy, you are better equipped to resist him and his wiles. He wants to intimidate you. He wants to deprive you of everything that belongs to you. If you cave in, you could get run out of the Promised Land. It's time to stand up and take authority.

Take Back What the Enemy Has Stolen

Christians today are losing their way because of *intimidation*. It's time to declare war on the enemy. Everything the devil took from you on the other side of Jordan, you can take back when you get to the Promised Land. The Promised Land belongs to you. All the benefits are yours.

You can take authority over sickness. Sickness and disease have lost their power, but sickness can attack you if you're not saying anything. It's time to declare, "I'm a Promised-Land dweller. I will not let sickness overtake my body. In the name of Jesus, *get out of my body.*"

Take Back Your Finances

In the exact same way, you can take authority over poverty and lack. Everything you need is in the

Promised Land. You should lack nothing. Poverty can't stay in your life when you dwell in the Promised Land. Don't be satisfied with barely enough. God wants to bring you into the land of more than enough. Riches and wealth belong to you. Follow God's instructions:

> **Bring ye all the tithes into the storehouse, that there may be meat in mine house, and prove me now herewith, saith the Lord of hosts, if I will not open you the windows of heaven, and pour you out a blessing, that there shall not be room enough to receive it.**
>
> **Malachi 3:10**

You may be in a situation where you can't pay your bills, and you think God is teaching you a lesson. Don't blame God for your lack. He has given you the authority in the Promised Land.

Take Back Your Good Name

Do you know a good name belongs to you? God promised to make your name great (Genesis 12:2). If the enemy tried to ruin your name a few years ago, you need to tell him, "You should have killed me while I was on the other side of Jordan. Now that I'm in the Promised Land, I've got a new name. My name is now *Promised-Land dweller*." See what he can do with that piece of news!

Take Back Your Purity

For others of you, the devil stole your virginity while you were on the other side of the Jordan. You may have had children out of wedlock. But now that you've come to Jesus and you've repented, now that You've changed your ways and you mean business with God, He's led you into the Promised Land. Now the devil's trying to tell you, you can't get a husband. Tell the devil you left that old person on the other side of Jordan. When you got to the Promised Land, you became a virgin *all over again.*

Take Back Your Career

There are those of you employed beneath your potential. You've been taking little jobs for which you're overqualified. There's no need to settle for that. You may work there while you're looking for something better, but don't get comfortable there — it's only a stepping-stone. God wants to promote you. You're living in the Land of Promise and that means you're qualified. Take authority over your career and don't let the devil intimidate you. You've been passive for too long, saying you are humble. But humility doesn't mean you allow the devil to have free reign. If the devil is running you out of the Promised Land, he is invading your territory! Are you going to sit back and let him run you out of the inheritance your Father left you? **The devil is a liar.**

Take Back Your Marriage

You can take authority in your marriage. On the other side of Jordan, the devil may have stolen the joy from your relationship. He stole the love. He stole the romance. He stole the peace and contentment. The good news is, you are no longer in Jordan. It's time to take authority over your troubled marriage. Call back the love, the mutual respect, the trust and the romance. If you are a hurting spouse, God wants to turn that relationship around. Begin to believe Him for the answers you need.

Take Back Your Dreams

Finally, on the other side of the Jordan, you may have lost your dreams. You may have lost your vision. You may have lost your goals. Satan told you, "You'll never amount to anything." He's tried to make your future look bleak. But that's the same Satan who said you would never make it into the Promised Land. But where are you now? You're in the Promised Land! You took that step, and God brought you over.

The same God who brought you through Jordan into the Promised Land, is the same God who can control all your tomorrows and bless you. It's time to become all you've dreamed of being...all God wants you to be...receive all God wants you to receive.

You were made in His likeness. You were created in His image. Take your future back. Take your dignity back. Take your answer back. Take your courage back. You're a Promised-Land dweller.

Summary

When God tells us to be strong, He means for us to take authority. We are to come into the Promised Land and take back all that the devil has stolen from us. God wants you blessed, but Satan wants you cursed. Tell the devil it's too late. You've made it into the Promised Land, and you have taken authority in your land.

4

Prolonging Your Stay in the Promised Land

In chapter 3, we discussed the warfare that greets us in the Promised Land and how we are to take authority. Now in this verse we learn that God wants our stay in the land to be an extended one:

> That your days may be multiplied, and the days of your children, in the land which the Lord sware unto your fathers to give them, as the days of heaven upon the earth.
>
> Deuteronomy 11:21

Our days in the Promised Land are to be multiplied. But how can we be assured of this long stay? Let's look first at the importance of reliable leadership.

Following the Priests

> And it shall come to pass, as soon as the soles of the feet of the priests that bear the ark of the Lord, the Lord of all the earth, shall rest in the waters of Jordan, that the waters of Jordan shall be cut off from the waters that come down from above; and they shall stand upon an heap. And it came to pass, when the people removed from their tents, to pass over Jordan, and the priests bearing the ark of the covenant before the people;
>
> And as they that bare the ark were come unto Jordan, and the feet of the priests that bare the ark

were dipped in the brim of the water, (for Jordan overfloweth all his banks all the time of harvest,)

That the waters which came down from above stood and rose up upon a heap very far from the city Adam, that is beside Zaretan: and those that came down toward the sea of the plain, even the salt sea, failed, and were cut off: and the people passed over right against Jericho.

And the priests that bare the ark of the covenant of the Lord stood firm on dry ground in the midst of Jordan, and all the Israelites passed over on dry ground, until all the people were passed clean over Jordan.

Joshua 3:13-17

Prior to moving into the Promised Land, the Lord showed Himself to the children of Israel through signs and wonders. In the wilderness He used the pillar of cloud and the pillar of fire. Now God changes His style and methods, as He begins to use a prophet.

They are told to watch the priests, and when they move with the ark of the covenant into the water, follow them. They were to follow the priests into the Jordan River. And we know from reading the rest of the passage, that as soon as the priests stepped into Jordan, the whole of Jordan dried up. This allowed the children of Israel to cross over on dry land.

In order for Christians to cross over into the Promised Land, they must have pastors and leaders who have crossed over. If you're in a church where the pastor has no vision to cross over Jordan, you need to run for your life. The deliverance of the children of Israel depended solely on the vision and courage of these priests. It wasn't until the priests stepped into the

Jordan, that Jordan dried up and the others were able to enter the Promised Land.

Leaders Who Are Not Called

Many Christians today are committed to Jesus and are actively working in their churches, but they aren't going to make it into the Promised Land because of the lack of vision of the pastor.

> **Where there is no vision, the people perish: but he that keepeth the law, happy is he.**
>
> **Proverbs 29:18**

This familiar passage from Proverbs says it's the people who will perish. Because if the pastor has no vision to lead the people into the land of promise, the followers will never make it. The devil will make sure the people are settled and comfortable dwelling on the wrong side of Jordan.

Unless and until God moves through the hearts of His leaders, many people in the Body will remain defeated and wandering in the wilderness. In order to lead a church, a pastor must be called. I've seen people get mad at their pastor, walk out and start their own church or ministry without a vision from the Lord.

I address this issue in hopes that a pastor, or church leader, who has never been called of God, might heed this admonition. If you're not called to your position, if you have no vision to lead your people over into the Promised Land, it's time to go and apologize to God! Confess your sin for calling yourself into the ministry and ask the Lord to lay His hand upon you and show you how to get into the Land of Promise!

It takes a Promised-Land dwelling pastor to lead the people into their own Promised-Land experiences.

The Wilderness Is Character School

> Behold, I go forward, but he is not there; and backward, but I cannot perceive him:
>
> On the left hand, where he doth work, but I cannot behold him: he hideth himself on the right hand, that I cannot see him:
>
> But he knoweth the way that I take: when he hath tried me, I shall come forth as gold.
>
> Job 23:8-10

When you're going through the wilderness, it's as though God hides Himself from you. This is because He's putting you through "character school." God is writing the examination for your test, and He doesn't want to be readily available or accessible. He loves you so much that when He sees you suffering, He might write the answers to your test.

Job tells us when he was going through character school, he looked all around and couldn't find God. Even so, Job was still aware that God was present, and that He knew Job's situation. **He knoweth the way that I take, Job said** (v. 10). But then the test was over (when I am tried), faithful Job graduated with honors (came forth as pure gold). God is watching to see if we will continue to follow Him in spite of all the adverse circumstances which may surround us. Job made the decision to keep on following God's "steps."

> My foot hath held his steps, his way have I kept, and not declined.
>
> Job 23:11

That's how you get over Jordan — by taking that necessary step into the river following the priests and the ark. Remember, we ascertained that the Jordan was the place of warfare and the devil fights his biggest battles at Jordan. Whatever it takes, the devil will seek to keep you on the left side of Jordan to keep you out of the Promised Land. It is here that you will have the greatest trials and tribulations. The devil knows that when you get to the Jordan, all you need to do is take one more step and you'll be in the Promised Land.

Even Job's wife tried to keep him from crossing over (Job 2:9). But Job said, **My foot hath held his steps...** (Job 23:11). He remained steadfast.

Staying Behind at the Jordan

Neither have I gone back from the commandment of his lips; I have esteemed the words of his mouth more than my necessary food.

Job 23:12

In Job's case, obeying the commandments of God was more important to him than eating. Christians must be as determined as Job in order to make it across Jordan. Jordan is never permanent unless you agree to make it that way. If you sit back and relax, you'll get comfortable and never even get across. This is where many Christians are stuck — they've been sitting on the banks of the Jordan for years.

Why? They're content at having made it through the wilderness. They look back at the wilderness experience and see that God brought them a mighty long way. Things were tough back there in the wilderness. Now they've come to the Jordan, the place of warfare, and the devil starts fighting fiercely. So they make up their minds, "I've had enough. I'm not going through any more of this. I'm comfortable right here at Jordan. At least I'm out of the wilderness."

This explains why so many Christians are saved, sanctified, full of the Holy Ghost, and broke. That's why sickness can knock Christians down. You may be full of the Holy Ghost, because you made it through the wilderness, but you stopped at the Jordan. There are no blessings at the Jordan. The only thing at the Jordan is more warfare. At the Jordan, the devil is the master. People who camp there can see only what the devil shows them. Their vision is dimmed and blurred.

Christians parked at the Jordan may still be lying and cheating and scheming. They may be living in sin and not even feel convicted about it. This is why many backslidden Christians come back to Jesus in repentance, and the very next week they backslide all over again.

Teaming Up With Other "Jordanites"

To become even more comfortable, they find some other "Jordanites," and they connect. They become friends and they call themselves prayer partners. The only problem is, they're "Jordanite" prayer partners, and their prayers are going only as far as the brink of the Jordan. They don't have the foresight or the vision to see over into the Promised Land. The larger the group of "Jordanites," the more comfortable you will become.

Christians who live at Jordan are often "complainers." They're always complaining, because no matter what you have at Jordan, there's warfare.

God used Moses to lead the people out of Egypt, through the wilderness, got them to the Jordan, and then he died. He never stepped foot in the Promised Land. Likewise, many Christians will go into heaven without ever having experienced the Promised Land. They're perfectly satisfied being saved and on their way to heaven. They're singing, *"Wouldn't take nothin' for my journey now"* and *"I'm waiting down here at the river till You come, Lord Jesus."*

There's no need to wait at the river. He's already told us to take that step to cross over. Jesus is not coming to the river to carry us over. A Christian who is waiting for Jesus to transport him across will wait a long time.

Get connected with a pastor who is a pilgrim traveler on his way to the Promised Land. Keep your eyes on him and don't mind what they call him, and don't mind how they lie about him. When you see him take the ark of the covenant, you don't need to wait for Jesus. Jesus gave that pastor to you, and you can follow him and cross over. That's God's plan.

The more you study the Word, and the more you know the Word, the less sense some Christian songs make — such as the two mentioned above. That's why even the music ministry in a church should flow with the vision of the pastor. As the visionary pastor takes the church to the next level, the music must minister songs that are in agreement with God's Word.

God Knows Who Is Who

Personally, I've reached the point in my life and ministry where so many members of my church want to be in the Promised Land, I can't even afford to look back across the Jordan. There are a few of those who want to stay over there, living in sin, then come into church and lift up "holy hands."

But it doesn't matter how many hands you lift up, it doesn't matter how often you are a part of praise and worship, or how long you cry, or how much you pray.

If you choose to live the defeated life, the carnal life, then you can stay right there at the Jordan. Because the prerequisite for getting into the Promised Land is sanctification.

God knows who is who. More and more it will become obvious who has sold out to God and who has not. God's going to do some exposing and it will be very clear who crossed over Jordan and who stayed behind. The pastor can point the way, but he cannot force anyone to cross.

Referring back to the verses in Job 23, we find that while he was going through his test, Job wanted to stay totally focused on God's commands. Obeying God's commandments became more important to him than eating. This is an important key for moving forward into the Promised Land. Committed Christians are the ones who have developed an intense love for the Word of God.

The Promised Land Is Now

In the first chapter of this book, we stated that the Promised Land has often been referred to as heaven. But the Bible says that the Old Testament Promised Land was in the land of Canaan. Now I've been to Canaan. I went to Israel and I drove from Israel, through the wilderness, and on into Egypt — I did it in reverse from the children of Israel. So if we're talking about going into the Promised Land when you're dead, that means you're not going to heaven. You're going to Canaan. The Promised Land was not designed to be enjoyed when you're dead. We won't need milk and honey in heaven. If you're going to eat cornish hens stuffed with shrimp down here, do you want to be taken out of here to settle for milk and honey? As I indicated earlier, milk and honey represent the necessities and the extras.

The Promised Land is meant to be enjoyed on earth. And every believer is promised a Promised-Land experience. Right here. There's no waiting for the sweet by-and-by. In heaven, we'll be busy praising and worshipping.

It's amazing that some Christians are waiting to die and go where I've already been. Christians with no vision are in serious trouble. They want to wait for the Promised Land while the rest of us are enjoying the fruit of it today.

> All the commandments which I command thee this day shall ye observe to do, that ye may live, and multiply, and go in and possess the land which the Lord sware unto your fathers.
>
> And thou shalt remember all the way which the Lord thy God led thee these forty years in the wilderness, to humble thee, and to prove thee, to know what was in thine heart, whether thou wouldest keep his commandments, or no.
>
> Deuteronomy 8:1,2

We can see from this passage the exact reason God puts us through a wilderness experience. It is to humble us, and prove us, so He can know what's in our hearts. "Can I trust these people to live in the Land of Promise?" God asks. "I'll see if they'll serve Me when they have nothing!" That's what happened to Job. Job was put into a situation where he lost everything he had. And in the face of that calamity, Job still said he preferred God's commandments over his necessary food.

When we get into the Promised Land, God says:

1. We'll live,

2. He'll multiply all that we have, and

3. Everything in the land will be at our disposal.

Wilderness Lack Leads to Promised Land Blessings

We studied earlier about the abundance of water which the Lord says we will see in the Promised Land. He brings us into **...a good land, a land of brooks of water...** (Deuteronomy 8:7). Promised-Land dwellers will find water on the left, on the right, on the north, on the south, on the top and on the bottom. Everywhere you look, you'll see water — refreshing water.

Imagine coming out of the wilderness after forty years, and you've not seen a fresh stream of water for forty years. But now in this good land, everywhere you look, there's water!

We touched on this subject in the previous chapter, but now we'll explain in a bit more detail because God wants us to see the correlation here. He takes us through character school, which is the wilderness. If your lack and your challenge has been money, then you were put through a financial wilderness. You suffered from lack, want and poverty. But through it all, you continued to walk in God's will and follow His commands.

Now He can say to you, "Child, hold on! When you get into the Land of Promise, the one thing you won't have problems with is your wilderness-experience problem. Everywhere you look there will be money and provision."

Your wilderness challenge may have been in the marriage arena. Everything else in your life was going fine, but there's this husband, or wife who was running around. Strange phone calls came in the middle of the night; your spouse came in late or left for long trips with no explanation. But God told you to stand firm, to put all your trust in Him. If you stay in church and follow God's commands, when you get into the Promised Land, your mate will come around and your marriage will be whole again.

> **But they that wait upon the Lord shall renew their strength; they shall mount up with wings as eagles; they shall run, and not be weary; and they shall walk, and not faint.**
>
> **Isaiah 40:31**

Isn't that just like God? You cross the Jordan, God touches you, and He has a way of renewing your strength. He lets you mount up over that thing — the very thing that's been holding you down.

Watch Your Step

> **And the God of peace shall bruise Satan under your feet shortly....**
>
> **Romans 16:20**

> **For he [Jesus] hath put all things under his feet....**
>
> **1 Corinthians 15:27**

There are two ways to look at this word *step*. First of all, the Lord has told us, everywhere we step, or tread, belongs to us. Secondly, God told us the enemy is under our feet, so we are to step on him. We have the authority to walk on the devil's head. Any time he comes after me, he's under my domain, he's under my control, he's under my authority. Why? Because the devil is under my feet! Jesus placed Satan there. His death, burial and resurrection assure us that the devil has been defeated.

In this good land, there'll be brooks of water, fountains, springs in the valleys and up and down the hills. Everywhere you go you'll find water. That's our awesome God.

In verses 8 and 9 of Deuteronomy, chapter 8, it describes the land of wheat, barley, vines, fig trees and pomegranates; a land of oil olive, and honey; a land where you will eat bread without scarceness.

God never does anything halfway. When God says He'll fix it, it's well-fixed. God will never bring us into the land of barely enough. Rather, He will take us into the land of more than enough. There's bread enough to eat till you're full, then you can give some away, and throw some to the dog and cat. When you do, there'll still be more than you need. This good land is a land of *more than enough!*

Perhaps in this study I've not touched your area of need, because I realize the areas of need in the Body of Christ are diverse. But God has it all covered. It may not be a physical healing, or finances, or marital, but something totally different. It doesn't matter. God promises, **Thou shalt not lack anything in it**.

Pastors Lead the Way

God has set an order in the Body of Christ. The priests went into the Jordan carrying the ark. The people were to follow. As mentioned previously, pastors and preachers must be Promised-Land dwellers before they can lead in their congregation. There is a specific danger that lies in this area. Often, there is envy in the heart of parishioners toward a successful pastor whom the Lord is abundantly blessing.

Recently, my congregation blessed me with $20,000 for a car. I borrowed the rest to purchase two cars. As we were pulling the deal together, the man at the car dealership and I kept missing one another. One day I received a call from him, and I learned that he'd already licensed the car and inspected it. All I had to do was pick it up.

When I called the bank to see when the check would be ready, he said, "How long are you going to take to come and get this check? It's here and waiting." That's Promised-Land dwelling. As the pastor who is holding the ark of the covenant, and leading the people into the Promised Land, how can I lead if I have no testimony of Promised-Land dwelling?

The blessings of my people cannot exceed what I am experiencing. Every time the Lord blesses me, and I go to another level, it's time for my people to rejoice. When your pastor is blessed in a super-abundant way, it's time for you to say, "Oh, look what God has done for my pastor! Now I know what God is going to do for me."

This is no time to be envious — this is the time to rejoice!

In the same vein, this is a good way to observe a church you're thinking about attending. Check out the pastor, check out the membership, check out the church building. Is the pastor driving a broken-down car that barely runs? Does the church need painting? Are the floors dirty? If the leader allows the house of God to fall into disarray, you may question how his private life is being conducted.

In my home church, there should never be a bigger tither than me. Never. That's why every time I see God blessing my members I get excited. I brag on my people and rejoice and celebrate when the blessings flow! If I'm on a certain level and God blesses somebody and they get to that same level, then I'm about to be promoted. Because God set me as the leader of the congregation and I'm required to set the pace and lift up a standard among the people.

My Personal Wilderness Experience

When our church building was being constructed in Nassau, I literally went broke when the contractor milked us out of almost $100,000. The windows that were installed were paid for twice. More than $80,000 of my own money was pumped in to completing the building, and I've never even thought of asking the church for it back.

My wife and I had planned to use that $80,000 to renovate a house that we had bought not too long before. It was our own house, the church didn't buy it. When we used the money for the church instead, we lived in the house for five years just the way it was. As far as I was concerned, the house of God came first.

Then at a later time, in my due season, the Lord blessed me with an increased number of speaking engagements — He put me on the road preaching all over the world. People were blessing me abundantly. Eventually, I spent $110,000 renovating my house in one year's time. And I didn't have to go to the bank for a penny. That's our God of more than enough!

And some have the nerve to wonder how the congregation could bless me with $20,000 for a car. What's $20,000 against $80,000? But I've understood the

law of sowing and reaping for a very long time and I
know it works.

Beware of Envy

It's dangerous to let envy rise up in your heart
against your pastor. You have no idea what he's been
through. You have no way to measure what his wilderness experience may have been like.

People come into my nice office now and raise
their eyebrows. But when I first came to the church
full time, I shared a small office with a secretary. When
somebody came for counseling, I had to put the
secretary out. We worked in that office for two years
with no air-conditioning. And in the Bahamas, it can
get very warm. Then one year, on pastor's anniversary
day, the women's department presented me with a
little window unit air conditioner. To me, that was a big
improvement. Now we have nice offices with central
air-conditioning. When God brings you out, He'll give
you much more than you had previously.

Several years ago, I went through a time when
people wouldn't speak to me because of rumors and
lies. I had members within my church who believed
the lies. Members of my own family turned against me.
That was the wilderness experience! But now God had
blessed me with loyal people who believe in this
ministry and want to work alongside me.

Verse 10 of Deuteronomy, chapter 8, reminds us,
**When thou hast eaten and art full, then thou shalt bless
the Lord thy God for the good land which he hath
given thee.** No matter what God does for us, we are to

continue to love and serve Him because He gave it all to us in the first place.

Summary

The Lord has given us types and shadows in the miracle of crossing the flooded Jordan River. The people waited for the moving of the priests and the ark, and they followed that leading. But how can one cross the flooded Jordan if the leader is not willing to cross? If there is an able leader who has crossed over, how can the followers be blessed if they are busy being envious and jealous of the pastor's Promised-Land blessings? Watching your pastor be blessed should encourage your heart. After all, you're following his leading, so rejoice! Your blessings are on the way!

5

Rest From Your Enemies

The Enemy Will Try To Pull You Down

When entering into the Promised Land, it's always important to remember how desperately the enemy will try to keep you from partaking of all that is at your disposal. The following verses speak of rest from your enemies. This is a paradox, because this "rest" does not imply that Satan has given up or quit.

> But when ye go over Jordan, and dwell in the land which the Lord your God giveth you to inherit, and when he giveth you rest from all your enemies round about, so that ye dwell in safety;
>
> Then there shall be a place which the Lord your God shall choose to cause his name to dwell there....
>
> **Deuteronomy 12:10,11**

Here again, we find the important key word *when.* Now if you have already crossed over Jordan into the Promised Land, this future case of *when* no longer exists for you, because you're already in. When we are in, as you have noticed earlier, we build goodly houses and dwell in them. When we are in, our silver and gold are multiplied, and so on. In addition to all that, we're now told that we will have rest from our enemies.

What or who are our enemies? Please note that enemies are not always people. Sometimes enemies are things.

- Sickness is an enemy.
- Poverty is an enemy.
- Hard times and unemployment are enemies.

If you are of the age where you can be gainfully employed and you have energy and ability to do so, and yet you have no job, that's an enemy. But the Lord says you will have "rest from your enemy."

When an enemy is upon you, you can't concentrate. When an enemy is on you, it strives to pull you down to a lower level. When an enemy is on you, it wears you out — mentally, emotionally, psychologically, physically, and in many cases, financially. For instance, if you're sick, and you have to keep spending money on doctor bills, and perhaps losing money from time off work, the enemy is robbing you financially.

But the Bible says when you get to the Promised Land, God has a "rest" in store for you. This isn't talking about a nap or sleeping at night, although that kind of rest is important and vital to our health. But this refers to the rest that will give a sense of peace and well-being. It is the kind of rest that brings relief, where you will say, "I'm so glad I don't have to deal with that problem anymore." It's that kind of rest. "God, I'm so glad I got rid of that disease." "I'm so glad I'm out of poverty." "I'm so glad my marriage has been restored." There is a rest that comes from having been delivered.

Dwell in Safety

Deuteronomy, chapter 12, says not only will we have rest from our enemies, but it also promises we will dwell in safety. Earlier we studied about the promise that said we would dwell in goodly houses. God wants to assure us that we can dwell in them in safety, in spite of the high crime rates.

Criminals Are Enemies of a Society

There are criminals in the country who need to be locked up. I have little sympathy for criminals. I tell my parishioners if you do anything criminal, don't come to me, because I'll encourage the law to lock you up.

This has nothing to do with Christian grace or forgiveness. I'll pray for the Lord to keep you safe in jail. I'll even pray that while you're in jail, you don't give up on your salvation. But I will not cover up criminal activity. I'm not that kind of leader.

I also tell parents, "If your children commit a criminal offense, don't expect me to go down to the court and ask the magistrate for a favor." Whatever the law is, when a person breaks that law, that person should pay the price. Even as simple a thing as running a red light. If the police book you, go to court and pay the fine. If you're wrong, you're wrong. Don't try to cover it up.

This is happening in growing proportions in our communities: we cover up wrongdoing too much. This is one of the reasons crime and lawlessness are rampant in many countries. But Promised Land people don't do that, because there are a wide array of promises God has given to us, and we want to qualify for all of them.

One of these promises is that we will dwell in safety. God wants to protect us from the criminal element of society. With the crime rate as high as it is, it's easy to slip into fear. But Promised-Land dwellers need not live in fear.

Fear Is Not of God

> For God hath not given us the spirit of fear; but of power, and of love, and of a sound mind.
>
> 2 Timothy 1:7

> There is no fear in love; but perfect love casteth out fear: because fear hath torment. He that feareth is not made perfect in love.
>
> 1 John 4:18

Once you have arrived in the Promised Land, then the devil will try his best to intimidate you. If you succumb to fear, it means you are not taking authority. The enemy can put fear on you to the point where you're too frightened to go in your own house. God gave you a goodly house to dwell in, but you're frightened to stay there alone. Or you are dwelling in your goodly house, but you can't sleep because thieves are breaking in around your neighborhood. But that's in the *neighborhood*; that's not you. As a Promised-Land dweller, you should be able to go into your house, go to bed and go to sleep.

> I will both lay me down in peace, and sleep: for thou, Lord, only makest me dwell in safety.
>
> Psalm 4:8

> ...for so he giveth his beloved sleep.
>
> Psalm 127:2

God promises safety for you and your property — God is the Caretaker. If we are going to stand and believe for the things such as houses in the Promised Land, we must believe God for our safety. What's the use of having the house or car, or extra money, if we're not dwelling in safety?

Since 1995, I've served as the Bishop of Foreign Ministries for the F.G.B.C.F., a position which takes me away quite often on long trips. Years ago, I prayed with my wife, Patrice, and instructed her on how to get her spirit comfortable in staying at home alone while I was away.

"You live in the house which God through your husband provided for you," I told her, "and God helped us to build this goodly house. Now no devil can run you out of your house. When I'm away, you don't run down to your mother's. You don't live there. You are to stay in your own house."

For the entire fourteen years we've been married, my wife has never slept out of that house, unless we were out of town or out of the country together, or when she goes to women's retreats. When I'm away, if she's not with me, she's at home — dwelling in safety in the house God provided for us.

If you have a nice home on which you're paying the mortgage, are you going to stay at a friend's or relative's house because you're scared? That means fear has gotten a hold of you to the point where it runs you out of your own house. Fear is an enemy!

When you drive up in your driveway at night, do you look all around, twisting and turning and ducking? If someone is there, it doesn't matter whether you're looking around or not, so you just as well get out of the car and walk boldly into your house.

Now godly wisdom tells you to leave lights on. Leave lights on so you don't have to go inside in the dark, but there's no need to be afraid. Realize that fear is not of the Lord and make up your mind you will take authority over it.

Worship Where God Puts His Name

Going back now to the verses in Deuteronomy, chapter 12, it says, **When ye go over Jordan...** and we have done that. Once we've done that, we are promised we will have rest from our enemies and we will dwell in safety. God's eyes are upon you, and He is the Caretaker of your land. The next promise, in verse 11, is that **the Lord your God shall choose to cause his name to dwell there**.

When you select your place of worship, be sure it's a place where God chooses to cause His name to dwell. Our church in Nassau is called Mt. Tabor Full Gospel Baptist Church. "Full Gospel" tells who we are and what we believe. I almost renamed it "Promised Land Church." But because everyone in the area already knew it as Mt. Tabor, I didn't want to destroy that advantage of name recognition. But be sure you are attending worship services where God chooses for His name to dwell.

Pay Your Vows

> ...thither shall ye bring all that I command you; *your burnt offerings*, and *your sacrifices*, *your tithes*, and the *heave offering of your hand*, and all your choice vows which you vow unto the Lord.
>
> **Deuteronomy 12:11**

After the Lord has promised extensive blessings in the land, now He must issue a challenge. First, you make sure you have a place where you know God is and where His name dwells. Once you decide on that place of worship, then it is to that place where you will carry your burnt offerings, your sacrifices, your tithes, your heave offering, and where you will pay your vows. Nowhere else is biblically acceptable.

> **When thou shalt vow a vow unto the Lord thy God, thou shalt not slack to pay it: for the Lord thy God will surely require it of thee....**
>
> **Deuteronomy 23:21**

If you make a pledge to support your church, and you have no intention of fulfilling that pledge (or vow), then you should not make it. Cancel it or you will surely get hurt in the Promised Land, because the Lord requires us to pay our vows!

As a senior pastor, I have nothing to do with the money. When money is given to me, I hand it over to those who handle it. I never ask my congregation for a blessing for myself. If they want to bless me, the Lord will lay it on their hearts, and that's for them to receive blessings back. God has given me other avenues by which to live. Because of the gift He has given me to preach under the anointing, doors are always being opened for me to preach. Indeed, my gift makes room for me (Proverbs 18:16).

If the Lord tarries, all that you have pledged to give, and have given, will be multiplied back to you. But when you make a vow, God expects you to honor it. If you don't honor it, you are in sin. And when you do not follow the commands of God, it can cancel out your Promised-Land blessings.

Those Within Your Gates Are Blessed

> **And ye shall rejoice before the Lord your God, ye, and your sons, and your daughters, and your menservants, and your maidservants, and the Levite**

that is within your gates; forasmuch as he hath no part nor inheritance with you.

Take heed to thyself that thou offer not thy burnt offerings in every place that thou seest:

But in the place which the Lord shall choose in one of thy tribes, there thou shalt offer thy burnt offerings, and there thou shalt do all that I command thee.

Deuteronomy 12:12-14

In verse 11 he says, when you find the place where God is and where God has placed His stamp of approval, then take your offering there. In Biblical times, they had to bring live offerings to the temple. We're no longer in that dispensation. Our offerings are, for the most part, monetary. This is the freewill offering. That's what you give when the plate comes around. Then there are sacrificial offerings which are above and beyond the tithes. You are to bring all the tithes into the place where God has His name — into that storehouse (Malachi 3:10). However, if you don't pay your tithes, you have no measurement. How will you know when you've gone past the tithes in order to give an offering? And if you aren't bringing in the tithes, then you're not getting any windows opened.

The Bible says in verse 12 of Deuteronomy 12, when you bring your tithe and your offering, you shall rejoice. Why will you rejoice? Because those within your gates are blessed. This means as long as you're in the Promised Land, and you're doing what you're supposed to do. Your son could be strung out on dope and your daughter could get pregnant at sixteen, but they are under your blessings. It doesn't matter how things appear at this time. The fact is, you've crossed into the Promised Land, you're paying your tithes, you're bringing your offerings, and you're doing what God has instructed you to do. Even those who are employed by you will be blessed and they will rejoice, and they didn't have a thing to do with how you got into the Promised Land. Everyone within your gates will prosper because of you! That's Biblical.

In some homes, the husbands are still employed due only to the fact that faithful, godly wives are in that home. God's given those men employment in order to take care of that godly wife. But don't think the devil is going to continue to deceive them for the rest of their lives. You're in the Promised Land and you're praying for your unsaved husband — it's only a matter of time until he comes to his senses. He is within your "gates" and he is blessed.

Your children may be rude and ungrateful, but the devil can't harm them because you're in the Promised Land now, and they are covered under your insurance. Everybody within your gates is protected. Don't get too worried about what your children have to face in the world, because they're within your gates and they are blessed.

When they get outside of your gates, just going to school, they're still protected. The devil may try to come and put bad company around them and put evil-speaking people around them. But you keep bringing them to the house of the Lord where their spirits are being taught. The anointing of God will flow through them. Later, if they get into a bad crowd, God will make sure all the good teaching will come back to their memory.

Train up a child in the way he should go: and when he is old, he will not depart from it.

Proverbs 22:6

> But the Comforter, which is the Holy Ghost, whom the Father will send in my name, he shall teach you all things, and bring all things to your remembrance, whatsoever I have said unto you.
>
> **John 14:26**

Bring Tithes Into the Storehouse

Deuteronomy 12:13 warns that you are to be careful where you carry your tithes and offerings. You don't toss them out frivolously wherever you will. When you attach yourself to a church, your tithes belong there. No place else.

The same is true with your church attendance. After you become a Promised-Land dweller, you want to be very careful where you visit for worship services. There are a lot of "Jordanites" out there. If you're not careful, they'll grab hold of your spirit and bring you right back to the Jordan. And then when you go back to your Promised-Land church, you'll feel out of place.

Faithful Church Attendance

Another trap the enemy will use to pull you back into Jordan is guilt. It often happens when you invite a friend from another church to visit your church with you, the next week they make you feel like you must reciprocate. The solution to this problem is to invite the unsaved instead of inviting someone with whom you must reciprocate. Invite the unchurched. There are plenty of them out there. That way you won't be obligated to go to another church where they may be preaching "Jordan living" principles instead of teachings that would sustain you in the Promised Land.

> And let us consider one another to provoke unto love and to good works:

> Not forsaking the assembling of ourselves together, as the manner of some is; but exhorting one another: and so much the more, as ye see the day approaching.
>
> Hebrews 10:24,25

Your *tithes, offerings,* and *attendance* are all to be in the place where God has called you. If God is moving in a mighty way (which He will in a Promised-Land church), you can't afford to miss any services unless it's humanly impossible to be there. If it's through this church that He has delivered you out of Egypt and taken you into the Land of Promise and if your church is where God has placed His name, then this is the place to bring your offerings, your sacrifices, and your tithes. That means to also bring yourself. It says to "bring" the tithes. You can't "bring" them if you don't come along as well.

Summary

Fear is not of God. God's plan is that we live in our Promised Land in safety, and in peace, and free from the torment of fear.

God promises that in the Promised Land we will have rest from our enemies, but only if we fulfill the conditions. We are called to bring our tithes into the storehouse. When we do, there will be safety for all who live within our gates. When we are faithful to do all that God commands, He is faithful to fulfill all His promises to us. It's up to us to learn both the promises and the conditions for receiving them.

6

The Firstfruits

Truth Eradicates False Doctrines

In chapter 5, we discussed the importance of bringing tithes into the storehouse. In this chapter, we'll dig a little deeper into this important issue. When you spend quality time learning and studying about Promised-Land living, you will find that no longer will you be tripped up by man-made doctrines.

> And ye shall know the truth, and the truth shall make you free.
>
> John 8:32

The more truth a Christian learns from the Word, the less likely he is to be blown about by every wind of doctrine. I'm a Baptist, and I enjoy being a Baptist, but I am not bound by all their doctrine and tradition. I don't want to live in bondage.

> Be not carried about with divers and strange doctrines. For it is a good thing that the heart be established with grace....
>
> Hebrews 13:9

> Till we all come in the unity of the faith, and of the knowledge of the Son of God, unto a perfect man, unto the measure of the stature of the fulness of Christ:
>
> That we henceforth be no more children, tossed to and fro, and carried about with every wind of

> doctrine, by the sleight of men, and cunning crafti-
> ness, whereby they lie in wait to deceive.
>
> **Ephesians 4:13,14**

Previously we discussed the importance of keeping a vow to the Lord (Deuteronomy 23:21,22), and the
fact that when you obey the Lord, those within your
gates are protected. Regarding the tithe, we established
the fact that believers are to bring tithes into the storehouse. In other words, church attendance and tithing
go hand in hand. Let's look at what else the Word has
to say about the subject.

Doctrines of Foods

> But in the place which the Lord shall choose in
> one of thy tribes, there thou shalt offer thy burnt
> offerings, and there thou shalt do all that I command
> thee.
>
> Notwithstanding thou mayest kill and eat flesh
> in all thy gates, whatsoever thy soul lusteth after,
> according to the blessing of the Lord thy God which
> he hath given thee: the unclean and the clean may eat
> thereof, as of the roebuck, and as of the hart.
>
> Only ye shall not eat the blood; ye shall pour it
> upon the earth as water.
>
> **Deuteronomy 12:14-16**

There are a few man-made church doctrines which
deal with eating certain foods, or abstaining from
certain foods. But this verse clearly establishes that God
is not the author of those kinds of doctrine. Don't ever
abstain from eating something because somebody told
you that Christians shouldn't eat it. In other words, they
have made a doctrine of a certain food. If you do not eat
a certain food, it should be because you don't want it,

or because you don't desire that type of food. But not because of a doctrine.

The Scripture is clear: **Thou mayest kill and eat flesh in all thy gates,** *whatsoever* **thy soul lusteth after, according to the blessing of the Lord thy God which he hath given thee: the unclean and the clean...** (Deuteronomy 12:15).

Paul touched on this subject in his letter to Timothy:

> **For every creature of God is good, and nothing to be refused, if it be received with thanksgiving:**
>
> **For it is sanctified by the word of God and prayer.**
>
> 1 Timothy 4:4,5

If there is something that your soul desires, and you are not eating it, then you must be *fasting*. Fasting is when you deny the flesh of something you want, but in that case, you're doing something in the spirit realm. You're denying the flesh in a particular area, and this is a sacrifice you are making through fasting. But you don't go all through your life fasting — it's temporary.

Perhaps you came out of a particular denomination, and you've been taught all your life that you should not eat certain things. But now you're in the Promised Land. There's nothing that the Lord blesses you with that you should abstain from eating because of a man-made law. As I indicated earlier, if you abstain from a certain food, it should be because you don't want it, not because of a false doctrine.

God's Stipulation

The only stipulation the Lord makes in this

passage is that blood is not to be eaten. This is because God places great importance on the blood.

> **Only be sure that thou eat not the blood: for the blood is the life; and thou mayest not eat the life with the flesh.**
>
> Deuteronomy 12:23

Throughout Scripture the "scarlet thread" of God's blood covenant with His people runs clear and bright. References to blood sacrifices throughout the Old Testament are but types and shadows of Jesus' act of shedding His blood once and for all on Calvary.

In modern techniques of slaughter and butchering meat, all the blood is drained, so this is no problem in the meat we eat. The red we see is not blood, but rather the juice of the raw meat. However, there are cults which include the actual drinking of blood in their satanic rituals, which is in direct disobedience to the Word of God. The practice dates back to Biblical times. This is an abhorrence to the Lord.

Don't Eat the Tithe

In Biblical times, the wealth of the people was often measured in crops and livestock rather than money. Therefore, the instruction of tithing was in this terminology, speaking of herds, flocks, corn, wine, oil and so on.

If the people had to travel a long distance to the temple they were allowed to sell the cattle or sell the grain, and bring the money to the temple. The tithe was 10 percent of all their increase, whether it be in livestock, or oil, or grain.

> Thou mayest not eat within thy gates the tithe
> of thy corn, or of thy wine, or of thy oil, or the
> firstlings of thy herds or of thy flock, nor any of thy
> vows which thou vowest, nor thy freewill offerings,
> or heave offering of thine hand:
>
> But thou must eat them before the Lord thy God
> in the place which the Lord thy God shall choose,
> thou, and thy son, and thy daughter, and thy
> manservant, and thy maidservant, and the Levite that
> is within thy gates: and thou shalt rejoice before the
> Lord thy God in all that thou puttest thine hands unto.
>
> Deuteronomy 12:17,18

Those who were dwelling in the Promised Land were clearly instructed to take the 10 percent of the harvest out and not eat any of it. Take out 10 percent of the livestock, God instructed them. Take the tithe from out of the herd, but don't eat the tithe. They were not to eat the tithe in their houses.

When preachers begin to preach about money and tithing, the congregation often becomes uncomfortable. "Oh no, he's talking about money again." But this is a principle that will help Promised-Land dwellers to prolong their stay.

This is what the Word declares. When you work and receive your paycheck, don't negotiate anything with your tithe money. Don't even include that in your spendable budget, because it's not part of your income. Don't spend that tithe money within your gates.

Keep in mind, you are dwelling in the Promised Land and everything in that "good" land is yours. It's all yours. But if you're withholding from God the part that is due Him, how can He trust you with greater increases?

Going Forward or Falling Backward?

> **Take heed therefore how ye hear: for whosoever hath, to him shall be given; and whosoever hath not, from him shall be taken even that which he seemeth to have.**
>
> **Luke 8:18**

When a believer lives in disobedience, the Bible says the little which he has shall be taken away. The devil will come and whisper in your ear, "Since you're a little short this month, just cut back on the tithe and you can catch up next time."

Usually when that happens, you never catch up. This is how Christians bring curses upon themselves. Don't buy groceries with the tithe money. We think we can cheat on God and there's no harm done, but that in an indication that we are still living on the other side of the Jordan. Do you enjoy being able to cheat a little and get away with it? You've got to decide: Are you going forward or falling back?

Offerings as Worship

If Promised-Land dwelling is for you, then:

- Pay no heed to doctrines that pertain to food,
- Don't eat the blood, and
- Don't borrow (or eat) your tithes.

Beyond giving tithes, there is the freewill offering and the "vows" which you have promised to the Lord. The offerings are a part of worship. If you know you're on your way to worship, be careful not to spend your last cent. You know you're coming to church and all you have is $5 left, hold some back to give as an offering unto the Lord.

Paying tithes and giving offerings are just two more ways to ensure a long stay in the Promised Land. And it's imperative that you know what you're up against. The devil is a deceiver, and he will come and tell you, "You tithed just last week." Well, you've received another paycheck since then, so there's been another increase and the tithe is on your increase.

> Honour the Lord with thy substance, and with the firstfruits of all thine increase:
>
> So shall thy barns be filled with plenty, and thy presses shall burst out with new wine.
>
> Proverbs 3:9,10

Likewise, the enemy may tell you, "The church will never miss your little amount." You're right, your church will probably never miss your tithe. But to withhold it is to destroy your own standing in the Promised Land.

Bring the Tithe and Receive the "Meat"

The instruction, **But thou must eat them before the Lord thy God...** (Deuteronomy 12:18), relates to the other familiar passage on tithing which we've already cited:

> Bring ye all the tithes into the storehouse, that there may be *meat in mine house*, and prove me now herewith, saith the Lord of hosts, if I will not open you the windows of heaven, and pour you out a blessing, that there shall not be room enough to receive it.
>
> Malachi 3:10

In Deuteronomy we are told to bring the tithe before the Lord, and in Malachi we are told to bring the tithe into the storehouse. These two verses fit hand in hand and support one another.

A non-tithing person attends church only for the "gravy" — the good feelings. They may attend church on Sunday, but by Monday, the devil is slamming them around and they're living a defeated life.

The tithing person, on the other hand, attends church and receives revelation knowledge. Questions are answered, needs are met, problems are solved — all because of hearing the anointed Word of God. This is because the tithe was brought into the storehouse and God gave them "meat."

This is why two people can be in the same service and one will leave the way he or she came in, and the other will leave rejoicing in newfound knowledge. What is the difference? One brought their tithe and received meat, the other didn't bring the tithe, and all he or she received was gravy.

To eat it "before the Lord" refers to the place where the Lord has chosen to put His name, that's in the church — the storehouse.

When you bring the tithes and offerings into the storehouse, there are enough blessings to cover your sinning son, and your sinning daughter and all those who might be in your "gates." They are protected because you have meat in the "house."

Further, in Malachi 3:10, God refers to this as a way to "test" Him. The promise is that the windows of heaven will be opened, and there will be meat — the solid Word.

> **For when for the time ye ought to be teachers, ye have need that one teach you again which be the first principles of the oracles of God; and are become such as have need of milk, and not of strong meat.**

> For every one that useth milk is unskilful in the word of righteousness: for he is a babe.
>
> Hebrews 5:12,13

Deuteronomy 12:18 says we will **...rejoice before the Lord thy God in all that thou puttest thine hands unto**. When you pay your tithes faithfully, you are to enjoy the meat and celebrate, because you will be blessed, and you will be a blessing to others as well. Whatever you set your hand to do will be blessed (Deuteronomy 28:8).

As believers, most of us don't realize the power God has given unto us. Some businesses remain open only due to the fact that a believer is employed in their midst. God keeps that business open to bless that tithing believer.

Before I came into the full-time ministry, I managed four stores which were doing approximately $3.2 million in sales annually. Since I left in 1989, not one of them is open today. God's anointing was on me for the success of that business. When I left, it followed me to Mt. Tabor. That's why I can tell you we need to take the authority in the Promised Land.

If you're a good worker and you're committed and there's been no raise in your salary, it's time to have a talk with your employer to find out why. It's time to take authority in the Promised Land. I've been there and I know God is faithful to His Word.

Forsake Not the Levite

> Take heed to thyself that thou forsake not the Levite as long as thou livest upon the earth.
>
> Deuteronomy 12:19

The Levite is equivalent to the pastor in your church. The pastor is not supposed to go to people to ask that they take care of him. Why does it say to take heed to thyself? Because how you care for your pastor will come back on you. This is God's warning and admonition. The same God who tells you to take the step to cross the Jordan, tells you to take heed to care for the Levites, or the pastors. People in a church who never bless their pastor are showing their Jordan behavior. Promised-Land dwellers "take heed" to bless their pastors.

However, keep in mind that parishioners will not be Promised-Land dwellers if the pastor is not a Promised-Land dweller.

You should have to strive to get to where your leader is. If you're beyond him, how can he lead you? If you're beyond him, then you must be leading.

When the pastor is beyond his congregation, then those who are tithing will not be able to exert undue pressure on him — or seek special favors. I've heard of churches where the tithers control everything. They tell the pastor what to preach and what not to preach. And the pastor is so scared of losing their tithe money, he submits to their control. A pastor who is enjoying Promised-Land benefits will tell those types of people to take their tithes and move on to another church, because he/she will not be controlled by anyone, other than the Holy Spirit.

Now what does the Lord promise right after the admonition to take care of the pastor?

> **When the Lord thy God shall enlarge thy border, as he hath promised thee....**
>
> **Deuteronomy 12:20**

God wants to enlarge their borders — or in other words, give them more than they presently have! Christians who don't take care of their pastors block their own blessings. When you take care of the pastors, then the Lord promises to take care of you.

Battling the Enemy

> **When thou goest out to battle against thine enemies, and seest horses, and chariots, and a people more than thou, be not afraid of them: for the Lord thy God is with thee, which brought thee up out of the land of Egypt.**
>
> **Deuteronomy 20:1**

In chapter 5, we discussed this problem of fear of the enemy. Here the Lord tells us to be not afraid of the enemy — even though there are more of them, and even though they are well-equipped with horses and chariots.

> **Some trust in chariots, and some in horses: but we will remember the name of the Lord our God.**
>
> **Psalm 20:7**

The enemy may need special equipment, but all we need is to obey God and trust in Him.

We are still discussing the way to stay in the Promised Land, and that is to bring your tithes into the storehouse — which is obedience. Returning to the book of Malachi, we see that God gives a special promise to those who are obedient to tithe:

> **And I will rebuke the devourer for your sakes, and he shall not destroy the fruits of your ground; neither shall your vine cast her fruit before the time in the field, saith the Lord of hosts.**
>
> **Malachi 3:11**

Importance of Collective Worship

> And it shall be, when ye are come nigh unto the battle, that the priest shall approach and speak unto the people.
>
> Deuteronomy 20:2

When Christians go into battle, the support of the Body of Christ is imperative. When we stand alone, we become an easy target for the enemy to pick us off. But collectively, when we stand together as a united Church Body, it's much more difficult for the enemy to take us down.

Deuteronomy 20:2 explains that when we come unto the battle, the priest will speak unto the people. This can be likened to the pastor speaking to his congregation as they face the battles of daily life.

We need to take our church attendance far more seriously than we do. The saints of God need to understand the reasons why we come to church. It's not just for a pastime. If we truly understood how important it is to join in corporate worship, and to hear from the man of God, then we wouldn't stay home to do the laundry or wash the car on the Lord's day.

We come together to receive a word from the Lord. And God chooses to use your pastor. As a pastor, I take this responsibility so seriously. People who really know me know that I hardly go to sleep on Saturday nights. I want to pray and listen throughout the hours of the night so I will be sure I hear what God is saying to me to speak to the people He has given into my care.

God will use your pastor to speak to you to prepare you to face your battles. But here's what happens. If you are not in your place — you stayed home to sleep in, or catch up on the chores — that could be the very time that the priest has a word from God for you. Then next week you come all messed up spiritually, you're battered, bruised and torn, because you were not in your place when the priest gave the instruction and the enemy got the upper hand.

Your pastor stands in a position of being God's mouthpiece for you. If you cannot see your pastor as your spiritual father and leader, then you need to find a new church. If you look at him and think to yourself, "He's just a man, I don't have to listen to him," then how can you receive and learn from him?

Since we have battles to face every week, we need to take whatever opportunity we can to be in the house of the Lord, where the priest is going to speak God's word for the hour. You want to be there to get your ammunition, so when the devil comes with his attack, you're equipped and ready. You can say, "You should have caught me before I went to Bible study last night. But now I know — I have my word from the Lord, and you're a liar, devil."

This is why it's so important that you be in your place of worship whenever you possibly can.

God Fights Our Battles

> And shall say unto them, Hear, O Israel, ye approach this day unto battle against your enemies: let not your hearts faint, fear not, and do not tremble, neither be ye terrified because of them;

> For the Lord your God is he that goeth with you, to fight for you against your enemies, to save you.

> **Deuteronomy 20:3,4**

Now if you knew for certain that the Lord was going to fight your battles for you, you wouldn't faint. You wouldn't tremble.

I have eight brothers and I'm the seventh child. So when I was growing up, I used to show off and pick fights. I could pick a fight with other boys, because I knew I wasn't going to have to fight against them alone. Anyone who messed with me was an idiot. With my big brothers all standing around, how could I lose? They were right there to fight that battle for me. There was no way I could lose. If I picked on someone my own size and my brothers were bigger, how were they going to beat me and my brothers? I picked fights where I was certain of the victories.

When you're in a battle facing the enemy, and you know before the fight starts that God will save you, you won't tremble, you won't be fainthearted, you won't be full of fear.

Remember To Be Thankful

> And the officers shall speak unto the people, saying, What man is there that hath built a new house, and hath not dedicated it? let him go and return to his house, lest he die in the battle, and another man dedicate it.
>
> Deuteronomy 20:5

Remember, we learned that when we arrive in the Promised Land, God is going to give us goodly houses. Verse 5 reminds us that those houses are to be blessed back to Him. This verse refers to this as "dedicated." This is a warning not to become ungrateful. He's saying, "Before you go into any battle with the enemy, get down on your knees and thank God for that home

— and all your blessings." You don't want to be found facing an enemy when you've been ungrateful for all that God has already given you.

> And what man is he that hath planted a vineyard, and hath not yet eaten of it? let him also go and return unto his house, lest he die in the battle, and another man eat of it.
>
> Deuteronomy 20:6

Here we find yet another analogy for blessing back to the Lord that which He has given. What kind of person would receive all this goodness from God and not be full of thanksgiving? The Promised Land is filled with abundance, but we are not to forget where it comes from and the Source of all our blessings. **...For unto whomsoever much is given, of him shall be much required...** (Luke 12:48).

Bringing our firstfruits (tithes) into the house of the Lord is part of our demonstration of thanksgiving and gratefulness.

Summary

It's not the Lord's will that we get caught up in man-made doctrine about external things such as eating certain foods. As our knowledge of the Word increases, we will not be susceptible to all the "winds of doctrine" that may blow about us. We are promised that we will have "meat," or the solid Word of God, when we bring our tithes into the storehouse. To those Promised-Land tithers who also give offerings to bless and support their pastor, God promises to enlarge their borders.

The Lord also admonishes believers to be a part of

corporate worship where we are to receive that "meat" from the pastor whom God has appointed over us.

Thanksgiving and a grateful heart are important ingredients of Promised-Land dwelling. Nothing we have done, or will ever do, can qualify us for this land which flows with such abundance. It is only because of a loving, caring God, and therefore, we must continue to give thanks to Him for it all.

7

Overtaking Blessings for Promised-Land Dwellers

Losing the Battle By Default

Thus far in our study of Promised-Land dwelling, we've learned that we must take the step to go over the Jordan into the "good land." There are many promises in that land, and yet the enemy will be there to deceive us into thinking we don't deserve, or we don't qualify, for all those blessings. As a result, there are many Christians in the Promised Land who will not take authority and will not claim what is rightfully theirs. But whether they take it or not, it is their rightful inheritance.

> And it shall come to pass, if thou shalt hearken diligently unto the voice of the Lord thy God, to observe and to do all his commandments which I command thee this day, that the Lord thy God will set thee on high above all nations of the earth:
>
> And all these blessings shall come on thee, and overtake thee, if thou shalt hearken unto the voice of the Lord thy God.
>
> Deuteronomy 28:1,2

God is looking for a people whose hearts are set on serving Him and pleasing Him. This does not mean we are mistake-free, or that we've arrived at any stage of perfection. It only means that for all intents and purposes, we live our days allowing the rules of God and the laws of God to govern our lives. We may slip, we may make mistakes, but we are quick to repent. If this is your position, then the first phrase of this passage applies to you: **It *shall* come to pass....**

Following that phrase comes the big, two-letter conjunction "if." It's easy to ascertain if we are satisfying the "if." Because as a result of meeting that requirement, all that comes after belongs to us.

You can say to yourself, "I know that to the best of my ability I'm seeking after God and obeying His Word. Since I qualify for the 'if,' then all these promises which are listed belong to me." Saying it aloud helps to fortify the truth within your spirit.

If the truth is not settled inside of us, then we will continually allow the devil to cheat us out of all that belongs to us. We are being cheated mentally because the greatest battles are in our thought life.

You may think that if you make mistakes in your walk with God, that you've been knocked out for good. And so you lie there and refuse to get up before the count of ten. Consequently, you're losing out by default on some of your promises.

You can't get to the point where, because of a mistake in your life, you refuse to get up and respond before the bell. You're living in the Promised Land and that means the land is loaded with promises that belong to you when you meet certain conditions.

Mistakes vs. Rebellion

Understand that if you mess up while you're in the Promised Land, you don't necessarily have to be put out of the land. The way to be put out is if you become stubborn and rebellious. It was rebellion that kept the children of Israel out. Those who were stubborn and stiff-necked died in the wilderness. Rebellion means you don't want to repent and work to fix your problems.

If you are sinning and you continue to commit the same sin over and over, it becomes a mockery of God.

> **Be not deceived; God is not mocked: for whatsoever a man soweth, that shall he also reap.**
>
> **Galatians 6:7**

To continue to sin with the thinking that "God is faithful and just to forgive" is a dangerous position to be in. We are not to presume upon God's grace.

When we make mistakes and slip inadvertently, or take hits that come at us from the enemy, we may find ourselves knocked into the corner. If we fail to get up and respond for the next round, we lose by default. Even if your opponent is reeling and about to crash any minute, he will win. Why? Because he is standing and you won't get up.

Sometimes, even in the Promised Land, you will get bruises, because the enemy is still ever present. And the enemy comes up with attacks for which we are not prepared. Keep in mind, we have an enemy who does not know about fighting fairly. If he finds an opportunity to hit below the belt, he will do that. We are not exempt from knockout punches. What we need to do is make sure we have enough strength and enough ammunition to fire back.

Don't make the mistake of thinking that because you are now in the Promised Land, it will be smooth sailing all the way. What it does mean is that you are in a land where you will lack nothing. You are in a land where God will fight the enemy. You are in a land that God oversees and cares for Himself. You are in a land where God keeps His eyes on you, but that does not mean that you are exempt from the wiles of the enemy.

"It Shall Come to Pass"

However, in the midst of that warfare, **it shall come to pass.** *It shall come to pass.* Whatever God promised that you will have in the land, no matter how the circumstances appear, it shall come to pass, providing you meet the conditions.

Things may look bleak and hopeless for you just now, but the Word says, **It shall come to pass.** Based on what you're going through today, it may not look like you're even *in* the Promised Land, **but it shall come to pass.** Based on the problems and challenges you've faced during the last few days or months, it may seem as though since you arrived in the Promised Land, you've taken two steps backwards. But I challenge you to get it in your spirit, **It shall come to pass...all these blessing shall come on thee....**

If you hesitate, if you're unsure, if the noise of the enemy is stronger than your knowledge of the promises, then all will be lost by default. The enemy will continue to bluff you out. But remember, **...For in due season we shall reap, if we faint not** (Galatians 6:9).

God's Due Season

Everything in God's planning and in His system must happen in due season. Have you ever wondered how to know when due season is near? It's when the enemy throws some of his best assault weaponry against you. Is your back right up against the wall since you got in the Promised Land? Have things begun to look pretty bleak? Does the environment around you look like anything but the Promised Land? Then you're pretty close to your due season.

It doesn't matter what happens in your life, when due season arrives, there's no one who can stop your due season. I don't care how they talk, or how they lie. I don't care how they try to hold you down, or hold you back. The Word says, **...It *shall* come to pass....**

Get it in your spirit. Say it to yourself. Speak out whatever that thing is deep in your spirit, that you've been waiting on from God, it's yours. Look at the devil and tell him, **It *shall* come to pass**. Promised-Land dwellers must believe that it is so. We can't afford to lose by default. Stand and take authority for every blessing, they are your rightful promises from God. When it comes to pass, then God says He will set us high above all nations of the earth (Deuteronomy 28:1).

Now you have to individualize that and say, "He will set me on high above all nations." We've already mentioned how this represents all the things that were outside of your reach on the other side of the Jordan — all those things for which it seemed you did not qualify.

God is saying He will do the setting up on high. We don't need to try to push ourselves. It may be a loan for which you were turned down on the other side of the Jordan. But when you cross over, and when you live your life according to the laws of the Lord, you will have it.

We need not pull down another person to make ourselves look good. God will give the promotion. When

He promotes, not only will we qualify for that for which we don't deserve, but we will be set above those who were so sure we wouldn't make it — and those who attempted to thwart our way.

It's high time for us to see ourselves in those positions. Envision it! Establish it in your spirit. If you're a Promised-Land dweller, stop eliminating yourself from these promises. You may be able to see God doing it for others, but it's time to see it for your own self, in your own particular situation.

The truth of this teaching could change the way teenagers look at themselves, and how they view their futures. Some have been told they aren't worth anything, and that they'll never amount to anything. But God gives His solid promise that promotion is coming and it belongs to *every believer*.

Potential in Believers

The reason the enemy lies to us and tries everything he can to stop us is because of the mammoth potential within each believer. No one can tell by looking at us what vast potential we hold. It's not apparent in how we appear to others — it's hidden inside each person. God has given us a body as a frame to protect the potential. The seed God deposited in you has been wrapped up in a body so no man can touch it. Potential goes way beyond what other people see.

The problem is, the devil is killing the seeds before they have a chance to bud and grow. And for some, he's killing the seeds through default, because that believer is unable — or unwilling — to catch a vision of the potential God placed within them.

Overtaking Blessings

> And all these blessings shall come on thee, and
> overtake thee, if thou shalt hearken unto the voice of
> the Lord thy God.
>
> Deuteronomy 28:2

One day as I was traveling through traffic on my way to my office at the church, God gave me an analogy for this verse which aptly describes what it means to be overtaken by a blessing. I passed a bus, and then pulled over in front of it. After passing, the Lord showed me that my car represented a blessing. The other vehicles on the busy highway represented multiple blessings. Even though my vehicle (blessing) passed the bus, there were other vehicles (blessings) behind, coming up close. One blessing overtook (passed) me, and another was coming up right away. In the opposite lane, other blessings were zipping by all the time.

Some Christians are so busy analyzing their neighbor's blessings they miss what's right beside them. You're thinking, "How could God do that for her or him, and not for me?" Dwell on that negative thought for a while and soon you'll be thinking you're "less blessed" than that other person. That's a lie of the enemy. Beware of that trap, because there are blessings enough for everyone.

Some blessings don't stop when they overtake you. It isn't staying. When my car passed the bus, it didn't stop, but kept right on going. Some blessings aren't meant to be kept, but are meant to be passed on to others.

Here I am so blessed that I'm not even anticipating another blessing, and God says, "I can't wait for you to anticipate, because the level that I'm moving on, I can't even wait for you to find time to appreciate. So I have to overtake you, because not every blessing I put on you is for you to keep."

God says He wants to surround us with blessings. We're blessed already, but He will allow blessings to overtake us.

Keeping Blessings

When the "overtaking-blessing" comes along, we're to pass it on, and not keep it. That little blessing you receive, that was for you to minister to others. It came to you because God was getting ready to put someone in your path. God didn't want them to chip into what He had for you, so He overtook you.

He had to overtake you, because your due season for your next "keeping" blessing hadn't come up yet. But He was getting ready to bless someone whom He was going to put in your path. Therefore, God had to overtake you and get something in front of you.

If you don't pass it on, you could block or delay your due season. You get a little blessing and then you pocket it. If you're holding on to this little thing that God sent your way — which was sent to bless somebody else, then He can't give you the big blessing because your hands are filled with what wasn't yours to keep.

That's why God designed offerings. If you don't see somebody to bless, then offer it as a sacrifice. But don't keep it. If God can trust you with the "passing-on" blessings, then you're in a prime position for the "keeping" blessings. But if you can't handle a little blessing, how will you be ready for the due-season blessing?

You've got to be faithful in little things. When God is ready to really bless you, any small blessing will just get in your way. God will let that come and overtake you, so the other blessing can catch up with you. In the meantime, all those blessings on the other side are still moving in and out, running up and down. You are surrounded with blessings, but if you get "greedy" in the Promised Land, you'll miss out on your main blessings.

God Blesses All Types of Careers

> Blessed shalt thou be in the city, and blessed shalt thou be in the field.
>
> Deuteronomy 28:3

As I was praying about this passage of Deuteronomy 28, the Lord showed me an interesting correlation between this verse and the careers, or job positions, that we all hold. He told me that the city and the field represent two things: the city represents the white-collar jobs and the field represents the blue-collar positions where those people work with their hands.

The "city" represents the bankers, the doctors and the lawyers and those who work in the more professional careers. If you are gainfully employed in this type of position, God is going to bless you. Don't pay any attention to the businesses that might be closing around you. Don't even get the word *closing* in your spirit.

The "field" covers all the beauticians, the plumbers, the carpenters, the factory workers, and so on. You're blessed as well. Take this scripture and claim it as you awake in the morning and get ready to go to your job. Accept God's promise that you are blessed in the city and blessed in the field. No matter what type of employment you have, your career is blessed. He's set you on high!

Protection for Our Offspring

Blessed shall be the fruit of thy body....
Deuteronomy 28:4

The seed of a committed Christian couple, a couple sold out to the Lord, is very precious. That seed is also a threat against the enemy, and he will try every way possible to destroy it. There was a couple in my church who was trying to have a child, but she was having difficulty getting pregnant. During an anointed church service, I was led to pray for her. The prophecy came forth saying that within six weeks she would become pregnant, she would have a son, and he would be saved by age twelve.

Six weeks later, she came to prayer meeting and said she'd just been to see the doctor and she was six weeks' pregnant. She gave birth to a son, just as the prophecy was spoken. A year after the child was born, we stopped seeing the husband in the worship services. Later, they were divorced.

Now the actions of these parents cannot and will not negate the third part of this prophecy. The third part will still come to pass. But my point is, look how determined the enemy was to destroy this godly home and the marriage of this Christian couple. He is after our seed!

Let me give another example. The wife of one of our pastors was due to give birth. They are parents of two older daughters who were born before this couple came to know Jesus. Because of this, the wife, Ruth Ann, told her husband, "We must be very careful, because this is our first 'holy' seed."

She spoke great wisdom, knowing how desperately Satan wants to destroy holy seeds!

The Pastor's Dream

Before the birth, this pastor came to me to tell me of a dream he had about the birth of his child. He dreamt that he came into a room where my wife and I were standing. In his hand — the pastor's hand — he carried a fat, healthy baby. "In my hand," he said, "I was holding a slim, sickly-looking baby."

Now his wife, Ruth Ann, had been attending a public clinic all through the pregnancy. But a week or two before the delivery, she told her husband, "I'm going to a private doctor at Doctor's Hospital." Though he didn't know the reasoning behind her decision, the husband was sensitive and agreed with her. What he learned later was that this change made the difference of whether or not he would be allowed in the delivery room. At the public hospital, he would have been barred from coming in. At Doctor's Hospital, he was admitted.

The baby was a couple of days overdue and somehow it swallowed some of the amniotic fluid before delivery. Because of this, the child's respiratory system wasn't functioning correctly and there were definite breathing problems. It was a frightening few minutes, but the husband, being right there by his wife's side, went into warfare with the enemy. He prayed, "Whatever the devil is trying to do, in the name of Jesus, I cancel every plan and every tactic of the enemy."

My Dream

During this same time period, I too had a dream. God took me into the delivery room where Ruth Ann was giving birth. God showed me two scenarios. In the first scenario, He showed me that Ruth Ann's baby was stillborn. The child was born dead. But in the next scenario, I saw this pastor by his wife's side in the delivery room. He was in prayer, and the child was born alive and healthy. God had prepared this father to be a confident, Promised-Land dweller, taking authority and appropriating the promises of God in his life and in that of his wife and child.

Later, this pastor testified, "I believe there's a purpose for my son's life, and I purpose in my heart that I will present my child back to God. I'm going to give him like Hannah gave her son back to God in the temple to be used of God, because I believe there's a divine and ordained purpose for his life within the Christian ministry."

This was further confirmed by another prophecy which came forth saying that this child would accept Jesus as Lord and Savior before he turned nine years old.

These two corresponding dreams, and this attack of the enemy against this baby, spoke loudly to me that there is a war being waged over the seed of Christian couples. But in the Promised Land, God wants couples to know that their offspring are protected. Their offspring will be healthy and whole.

This victory with the pastor's child took place a short time after I had led our congregation into the Promised Land as a collective group. The Lord said to me that if I hadn't been obedient to lead them into the Promised-Land experience, the child would have been stillborn. And if this pastor had been absent and had not heard the truth about his position in the Promised Land, the child would not have lived.

The Lord spoke to my heart and said, "I shall give perfect offspring." God used this experience to teach us His highest desire for our seed. This promise is for the seed of Christian married couples.

For Promised-Land believers, whenever you learn you have become pregnant, you can go to the Lord and claim the promise that your child will be perfect in every way. Now this doesn't exclude the wisdom of proper prenatal care and good health practices. All promises are balanced in God-given wisdom.

Summary

There's a due season for Promised-Land believers and no one can stop that season from coming. Meanwhile, blessings are overtaking you which you are to pass on to others. God promises that your generosity will be rewarded.

God has promised to bless the work of our hands, no matter what our career choice might be, whether we are in the "city," or in the "field." Begin to believe that God wants your job, or your business, to be blessed abundantly.

It is time to take your stand and claim the promises of God. Because if you don't, if you are not on guard, the enemy will destroy your marriage and your children as well.

If you have lost a child to the enemy, it's time to prove the enemy wrong. Show the devil what a liar he is. Once you have crossed over Jordan into the Promised Land, you have every right to claim a healthy baby who is whole in every way.

This is your right and your heritage in the Promised Land. **Blessed shall be the fruit of thy body...** (Deuteronomy 28:4).

8

Taking Your Stand in the Promised Land

God Wants To Bless His Children

In order to fully understand our Promised-Land privileges, it's imperative we understand how much God desires to bless us and how desperately the enemy wants to keep us from those blessings.

> Now unto him that is able to do exceeding abundantly above all that we ask or think, according to the power that worketh in us,
>
> Unto him be glory in the church by Christ Jesus throughout all ages, world without end. Amen.
>
> Ephesians 3:20,21

There may be persons reading this book who are facing tremendous trials. I would remind you that God knows all about it. He knows who you are, where you are, and where you've been. I may not know what you're facing, but God does. And you need to be reminded that God also cares. You may be facing an illness, or a personal crisis; you may be worried, or heartbroken.

You may be under severe pressure, wondering, *"How am I going to make it?"* You may be trying to figure out how to stretch that paycheck in order to take care of the bills that just keep stacking up. Whatever it is, if it brings you suffering, if it brings you heartache and discomfort and pain, it's an enemy.

I encourage you to look the enemy in the eye and claim your Promised-Land promises. **Let God arise, let his enemies be scattered...** (Psalm 68:1).

A Christian's Steps Are Ordered of God

God has ordered your steps and it is not by accident that you are reading this book on Promised-Land living. With hundreds of teaching books on the market from qualified and anointed teachers, why did this book end up in your hands? I believe it's because you've come to the time in your walk with the Lord when you know you're at a crossroads. You've known there was more and now through this teaching, you've come to understand how to cross over the Jordan and obtain what is rightfully yours. You are not an afterthought; your steps are ordered of God.

> **The steps of a good man are ordered by the Lord: and he delighteth in his way.**
>
> **Though he fall, he shall not be utterly cast down: for the Lord upholdeth him with his hand.**
>
> **Psalm 37:23,24**

If you can receive the truths written in this book, you are about ready to cross over into the greatest victories of your life. You've been sowing, and now *it's harvesttime.* The devil also knows it and that's why he's been putting you through what you've been going through. That's why the devil has been fighting you the way he has been fighting you. The devil is afraid of your potential. He is afraid of what he knows God is getting ready to do.

Understand that the devil is not upset about what God has already blessed you with — he's worried about the blessings that are on the way.

- The devil is not worried about who you are, he is concerned about what you are getting ready to become.

- The devil is not upset by how God moved in your life last year, he is upset about how God is getting ready to move now.

He's desperately, frantically, trying to prevent you from knowing what belongs to you. He wants to intercept God's plan for your life. That's what your car accident was all about. That's what your illness was all about. All the things you've been facing and going through, the devil has been trying to get rid of you. He wanted to wipe you out before you had a chance to learn the truth.

But now it's too late. Because now you know. You know and understand what is yours in the Promised Land. You know how to cross over, and you know the conditions and stipulations God has given about dwelling there. You know that God has given you life, blessings and safety. Because of this knowledge, you're through listening to the lies of the enemy without fighting back. If you submit to the anointing of God and cling to His Word, you can be walking in confidence and living in victory.

Learning to Let Go

All your heartaches, your sicknesses, your crises, your dilemmas and your burdens can be history as you learn to let them go. God will go before you to fight. To let it go means you aren't going to worry about it anymore. To let it go is to suggest that you're putting the situation into someone else's hand, and you have the confidence to let it go. To let it go suggests that you are yielding control of the situation over to someone else, and that Someone is bigger and better and more powerful than you and I.

He is qualified to handle your situation. He is the Caretaker of your Promised Land. Now if He can handle our situations better than we can, why are we holding on? God may allow things to happen, but we choose how we will walk through them. And always remember, you are not going through it alone. God is with you in the now of your challenges and problems.

A Right-Now, On-Time God

> God is our refuge and strength, a very present help in trouble.
>
> Psalm 46:1

A "present" help suggests we serve a "right-now, on-time" God. He is a God who knows what's going on in your life right this minute. He knows and feels and appreciates your dilemma — right now. Just when you need Him the most, He's right there beside you. And because He is a right-now, on-time God, that means everything in heaven, right now, is working on our behalf. That is an awesome thought. There are things going on in heaven at this very moment that have you and me included on the agenda. There is an incredible confidence and sense of security that we experience when we put our life in God's hands.

Put Your Life in God's Hands

The first phrase of Ephesians 3:20 says, **Now unto him**. It does not say, Now unto them. One of the problems we Christians have is that we trust too many people with our lives. We must come to the point where God has exclusive rights. If we are going to live victoriously, and claim everything that God has for us, we must be liberated from people's opinions.

When God speaks to us, we are tempted to run to people to see if they agree. Then we don't move unless certain folk agree with what God told us to do. If you want to hold on to what God has prepared for you, then listen to God and don't worry what others say. He wants you to come to the point in your life where you trust Him implicitly, in spite of what's going on around you. Why does He want us to do that? Because of the next phrase: **Now unto him that is able....** God alone is able! He is the Able One.

You may have friends and associates — you *need* friends and associates — but you don't need to put your life in their hands. Never put your life into the hands of someone who needs to have his or her life in the hands of someone else. Because if I put my life in someone's hands, and he puts his hands in Satan's hands, look where that could lead. I refuse to put my life in the hands of anyone when I'm not sure where they're attached.

Some girls lose their virginity because they put their lives in the wrong person's hands. If God is in control of your life, when the boyfriend tempts you, you will tell him a flat-out "no"!

When you understand that God is able, then you will trust Him with your life. God has a vested interest in your life, and He will fight to protect it. For some of you reading this book, with all you've gone through, the real miracle is that you are still here. God has preserved your life.

When you were in your backslidden condition, you could have lost your life, but God protected you. When you were out all night, going places where you shouldn't have been, right after you lifted up holy hands in church — by all rights, God could have wiped you out, but you're still here.

If you claim the name of Jesus, and claim Him as Savior and are willfully living in sin, it's a miracle you are still around. But God is protecting His investment.

Above Our Highest Aspirations

Now this God who loves us, and who is an "able" God, wants to do **exceeding abundantly above all that we ask or think**. God is a God of superlative degrees. He not only blesses us, but He has ways of blessing us abundantly. Think to yourself: what is the greatest thing you could ask God for? No matter what it is, our highest aspirations are never beyond God's power. He is superabundant, over and beyond; He's the God of more than enough and He stands ready to meet all our needs.

In Psalm 23, David describes God as giving to us until our cup runs over. It's time to step in and take hold of all that was outside of your reach before you crossed over into the Promised Land. God will give you the opportunity to occupy places for which you would not have qualified previously.

Think of everything the enemy told you that you were not good enough for. Now see God giving it to you. Giving in a way that is exceeding abundantly above all that you can ask or think.

You will walk through doors which heretofore were closed in your face. In the Promised Land, those doors will swing wide open. God is no respecter of persons. What He promises to one believer, He promises to all believers.

The weights and burdens you were dragging along in the wilderness can be left behind on the far side of the Jordan. It's time to let them go.

Let Go and Watch God Work

> **Come unto me, all ye that labour and are heavy laden, and I will give you rest.**
>
> **Take my yoke upon you, and learn of me; for I am meek and lowly in heart: and ye shall find rest unto your souls.**
>
> **For my yoke is easy, and my burden is light.**
>
> **Matthew 11:28-30**

To let go of your burdens is to say you are trusting the Lord to take care of the problems.

- Let go and watch God bring you the job you've been praying for.
- Let go and watch God bring that wayward husband back home.
- Let go and watch God multiply your finances so you can pay your bills and have money left over.
- Let go and watch God give you back your dreams which you thought had been dashed to pieces.
- Let go and watch God become your very present help in time of your troubles.

He'll change your darkness to light and your weeping to joy. Weeping comes in the night, the Word says, but joy comes in the morning (Psalm 30:5).

If your God was able to bring you out of Egypt and

across the Jordan, then He's able to keep you in your Promised Land! If He saved your soul, then He can deal with your problems. If God saved you from destruction, He can deliver you from your dilemmas. If God changed your heart, then He can change your home. If God changed your outlook, then He can change your outcome. If God fixed your yesterday, He can take care of your tomorrow. With God's strength behind you, His Spirit within you and His arms underneath you, in Him you have all sufficiency for the days ahead.

When the Way Is Dark

This is not meant to make light of the dark times in your life. It's not always easy to let go. Sometimes in the midst of all the lonely moments, sometimes in the midst of our broken hopes and shattered dreams, we become spiritually frustrated and exasperated. We are disappointed, disillusioned and distraught. Sometimes the way seems so dark, we're not sure where to go or what to do. We have no idea how we will have the strength to face tomorrow. But God wants you to know that He has special compassion on those who are near to fainting.

> He giveth power to the faint; and to them that have no might he increaseth strength.
>
> Even the youths shall faint and be weary, and the young men shall utterly fall:
>
> But they that wait upon the Lord shall renew their strength; they shall mount up with wings as eagles; they shall run, and not be weary; and they shall walk, and not faint.
>
> **Isaiah 40:29-31**

This is not a time to allow past failures to weigh you down. No matter how the past has looked, set your eyes on your Promised Land and allow yourself to envision all that God has for you.

Lift Up Your Eyes and Look

> **And the Lord said unto Abram...Lift up now thine eyes, and look from the place where thou art northward, and southward, and eastward, and westward:**
>
> **For all the land which thou seest, to thee will I give it, and to thy seed for ever.**
>
> **Genesis 13:14,15**

God promised to give Abram all the "land" that he could "see." What do you see? If all you see is Egypt and bondage, or wilderness and lack, then how can God give you all His blessings in your Promised Land? Let go of Egypt; let go of the wilderness. Cross over Jordan, come into your Promised Land, and you will begin to live up to the potential for which God created you. He has spread a table before you in the presence of your enemies (Psalm 23:5), but He will not force you to sit down and eat. That part is up to you.

Conclusion

It's simply not true that God wants you to wait until the sweet by-and-by to experience the good things of life. The Scriptures bear out repeatedly that God wants His will to be done on earth *as it is in heaven*. Therefore, there is a Promised-Land experience for every believer in Christ. But we must be determined to cross our Jordan and deal with every tactic the devil uses to try to destroy this experience by taking authority. Then we must do all God requires of us to prolong our stay in the Promised Land, because rest from our enemies and overtaking blessings are just a few of His provisions for us.

Finally, we must be prepared to take a stand and let nothing or no one move us out of our Promised-Land experience. Once you understand and have received these instructions into your spirit, you can begin your sojourn in your own Promised Land *this very day!*

About the Author

Bishop Neil C. Ellis pastors one of the fastest growing churches in the Bahamas. Located in Pinewood Gardens, Nassau, Mt. Tabor was started in 1987 with thirteen people. Today, the membership is more than 3,000.

Bishop Ellis has travelled extensively and has preached all over the Bahamas, the Caribbean, Israel, Germany, and the United States and has already given birth to a number of people into the ministry. Locally, Bishop Ellis serves on a number of Ecumenical and Civic Boards. Internationally, he serves as Regional Bishop for the Bahamas and Bishop of Foreign Ministries for the Full Gospel Baptist Church Fellowship with responsibility for hundreds of churches outside of the United States.

Because his life's ambition is to see men, women and children of all persuasions, live in victory and walk in authority, he has authored several books bearing the message of deliverance and abundant living.

Bishop Ellis, who believes in and places high priority on the family, lists his wife, Patrice, as his biggest human asset in ministry. His greatest desire is to see souls won into the Kingdom of God and live under the anointing of God.

TAPES

Single Cassettes - $5.00 each

A Word for the Righteous
A Pattern for Fathers
Acting Like a Fool
Living in a Mess
Walking in the Fire
How Much Can You Take?
How to Handle Persecution
A Prescription for Your Situation

2-Part Tape Series - $10.00

Seeing It Before You Get It
A New People
Understanding the "New Thing"
Tell the Devil, "Never Mind!"
Comprehensively Covered
Temptation
Tell the Devil, "I'm Still Here"
Standing Between My History & My Destiny
The Power of the Blood

4-Part Tape Series - $20.00

Now Unto Him
When You Listen to God

6-Part Tape Series - $25.00

The Party Crasher
Victory Through Knowledge
Living in the Promised Land
Walking in Prosperity

CHEQUES, MONEY ORDERS, VISA & MASTER CARDS ARE ACCEPTED.
(Please add an additional $5.00 for shipping and handling.)

Mailing Address:

Neil Ellis Ministries
P. O. Box N-9705
Nassau, Bahamas
Telephone (242) 392-3626